Music in East Africa

Music in East Africa

∽

EXPERIENCING MUSIC, EXPRESSING CULTURE

∽

GREGORY BARZ

New York   Oxford
Oxford University Press
2004

Oxford University Press

Oxford   New York
Auckland   Bangkok   Buenos Aires   Cape Town   Chennai
Dar es Salaam   Delhi   Hong Kong   Istanbul   Karachi   Kolkata
Kuala Lumpur   Madrid   Melbourne   Mexico City   Mumbai
Nairobi   São Paulo   Shanghai   Taipei   Tokyo   Toronto

Copyright © 2004 by Oxford University Press, Inc.

Published by Oxford University Press, Inc.
198 Madison Avenue, New York, New York, 10016
http://www.oup-usa.org

Oxford is a registered trademark of Oxford University Press

Library of Congress Cataloging-in-Publication Data
Barz, Gregory.
    Music in East Africa : experiencing music, expressing culture / by Gregory Barz.
        p. cm.—(Global music series)
    Includes bibliographical references (p.) and index.
    ISBN-13 978-0-19-514152-8 (pbk. : alk. paper)
    ISBN 0-19-514151-2 (cl : alk. paper)—ISBN 0-19-514152-0 (pbk. : alk. paper)
        1. Music—Africa, East—History and criticism. 2. Africa, East—Social life and
customs.
    I. Title. II. Series.

ML350.B37 2004
781.62'9676—dc22   2003060848

Printing number: 9 8 7 6 5 4 3 2

Printed in the United States of America
on acid-free paper

Contents

∞

Foreword

In the past three decades interest in music around the world has surged, as evidenced in the proliferation of courses at the college level, the burgeoning "world music" market in the recording business, and the extent to which musical performance is evoked as a lure in the international tourist industry. This heightened interest has encouraged an explosion in ethnomusicological research and publication, including the production of reference works and textbooks. The original model for the "world music" course—if this is Tuesday, this must be Japan—has grown old, as has the format of textbooks for it, either a series of articles in single multiauthored volumes that subscribe to the idea of "a survey" and have created a canon of cultures for study, or single-authored studies purporting to cover world musics or ethnomusicology. The time has come for a change.

This Global Music Series offers a new paradigm. Instructors can now design their own courses; choosing from a set of case study volumes, they can decide which and how much music they will teach. The series also does something else; rather than uniformly taking a large region and giving superficial examples from several different countries within it, case studies offer two formats—some focused on a specific culture, some on a discrete geographical area. In either case, each volume offers greater depth than the usual survey. Themes significant in each instance guide the choice of music that is discussed. The contemporary musical situation is the point of departure in all the volumes, with historical information and traditions covered as they elucidate the present. In addition, a set of unifying topics such as gender, globalization, and authenticity occur throughout the series. These are addressed in the framing volume, *Thinking Musically* (Wade), which sets the stage for the case studies by introducing those topics and other ways to think about how people make music meaningful and useful in their lives. *Thinking Musically* also presents the basic elements of music as they are practiced in musical systems around the world so that authors of each case study do not have to spend time explaining them and can delve immediately into the particular music. A second framing volume, *Teaching Music Globally* (Campbell), guides teachers in the use of *Thinking Musically* and the case studies.

The series subtitle, "Experiencing Music, Expressing Culture," also puts in the forefront the people who make music or in some other way experience it and also through it express shared culture. This resonance with global studies in such disciplines as history and anthropology, with their focus on processes and themes that permit cross-study, occasions the title of this Global Music Series.

Bonnie C. Wade
Patricia Shehan Campbell
General Editors

Preface

This is a book about people singing, dancing, and making music in contemporary East African communities. The primary themes of the book are the interaction of East Africans with traditional music and culture and the documentation of ways in which East Africans make music and dance useful and meaningful in their lives. The book has four main goals. The first is to contextualize the lives of individuals and communities by exploring the contexts in which music is made significant and integrated into the everyday experiences of East Africans negotiating the world around them. The second goal is to provide theories, methods, and case studies that enable access to the study of East African music traditions at multiple levels. The language of the theoretical arguments introduced in the volume is intended to invite rather than discourage engagement. The vocabulary and methodological framework is supported by the series' framing volume, *Thinking Musically*, and that volume's glossary supports many of the issues, concepts, and the terminology introduced in *Music in East Africa*. The accompanying CD complements and illustrates the several issues raised in *Music in East Africa*, providing opportunities for reading the more technical details of the text—musical notation, sound transcriptions, and analyses— at deeper levels. The text can, however, be read on different levels, and such technical exercises can either be adopted to the teacher's or students' individual level or disregarded. The third goal has to do with a defining principle by which musical characteristics of performance in East Africa can be distinguished, namely the inseparability and interdependence of drumming (and playing of other musical instruments), singing, dancing, and drama with traditional East African cultures. The tools for approaching this goal are embedded within case studies detailing the lives of individual musicians as specialized members of East African communities. A fourth and final goal is to encourage further research (historical or ethnographic) of East African performance traditions. The academic discipline of ethnomusicology is introduced in this text and from this exposure to the methodologies and techniques of ethnographic field research readers are encouraged to consider scholarly interpretations of East African materials as both process and product related directly to approaching meaning within performances of expressive culture. An overarching concept that arises throughout this volume's treatment of each of these four themes is *"traditional musical performance"*—three simple words that when grouped together refer at once to musical performance events, social phenomena, historical cultural trajectories, and the expression of individual and collective talent. Indigenous conceptualizations of traditional musical performance may differ among disparate and related peoples of this area of the world, with varying characteristics assigned to different aspects of performances of music, dance, and drama.

On finishing this volume I realized that I had tried hard to communicate something of the process I myself have engaged while conducting research in East Africa as I learned about the many roles assumed by music and dance in both historical and contemporary contexts. For me the engagement of this process will certainly be ongoing. I have lived, traveled, taught, and been taught in several areas of East Africa, and I have been fortunate to learn how to perform on many of the instruments introduced in this volume; I have danced many of the traditions discussed, and I have sung with East African vocal groups. As I conceptualized the case studies that form the core of this volume I returned to memories of being taught, memories of engaging and being engaged by my teachers, and memories of learning about and being exposed to East African traditional music.

Several languages are introduced in the text. KiSwahili appears most frequently, however, as it is widely understood and used in Kenya and Tanzania—but not so in Uganda. A largely Bantu-derived language, KiSwahili originated as the coastal East African lingua franca for Arab/Omani trading along the Indian Ocean coast as well as in the interior. When missionaries arrived in East Africa in the mid-nineteenth century, they often relied on KiSwahili rather than European languages for everyday communication. Stress in KiSwahili is almost always on the penultimate syllable (unless the word is of foreign origin). Thus, *"mwalimu"* is pronounced *"mwa-LI-mu."* Vowels are pure and for the most part standardized (a = ah; e = eh; i = ee; o = oh; u = oo).

The case studies that support this volume were written in Nashville, Tennessee, far away from the East African contexts of typical performances of music and dance detailed here, while the final draft was written in Kampala, Uganda, far from the context of my American classroom. Writing was an extremely pleasurable (and educational) task as it brought me closer to the valuable opportunities I have had to experience traditional music making, dating back to my initial field research in East Africa in 1993.

When I initially presented these case studies to undergraduate students at Vanderbilt University I came to realize that learning about music-as-cultural process equips students with a toolbox of ideas, concepts, and methodologies with which they in turn can approach many similar musical traditions in East Africa—traditional musical performances, popular music, choir music, dance music, and rap among others—and the rest of the world. An unintended product of the volume might well be, therefore, an opening of doors to curiosity and further learning concerning musics of East Africa as well as those of our own cultures.

ACKNOWLEDGMENTS

I am grateful to my many teachers, particularly Gideon Mdegella (Tanzania) and Centurio Balikoowa (Uganda). Mdegella and Balikoowa have become colleagues and friends; they are the musical experts from whom I have drawn much of my inspiration, and I only hope that I have done their teaching and guidance a degree of justice. Several East Africanist ethnomusicologists—Lois Anderson, Kelly Askew, Peter Cooke, Frank Gunderson, Jean Kidula, Gerhard Kubik, James Makubuya, Jeffrey Summit, and Sylvia Tamusuza, among others—have been eager colleagues and participants in my own education in this part of the world. Colleagues at Vanderbilt University's Blair School of Music—Dale Cockrell, Cynthia Cyrus, Melanie Lowe, Stan Link, Michael Rose, and Mark Wait—supported and encouraged the writing of *Music of East Africa*, and I am sure all will be greatly relieved to see the work published. Dennis Clark and the entire staff of the music library at Vanderbilt were tireless in their aid. Mona Christenson Barz continues to support and encourage my efforts. As spouse and field research assistant she has guided and inspired much in this volume.

This project was shepherded by the caring hands of Bonnie Wade, one of the general editors for the *Global Music* Series. Maribeth Payne, formerly of Oxford, provided initial support and encouragement, while Jan Beatty and Talia Krohn both guided the progress of the volume. Patricia Sheehan Campbell and Bryan Burton contributed insight concerning educational issues of much material in this volume. A wide variety of comments and suggestions from anonymous readers have been incorporated and adopted in this volume; I am grateful for all the time and energy they put into working through the volume's issues. Students at Vanderbilt University participating in World Music, African Music, and Afropop courses will find their comments (and critiques!) laced through the volume's cases studies.

Funding for the field research supporting this volume was provided by two grants from the Vanderbilt University Central Research Scholar Grants Program and a grant from the Fulbright African Regional Research Program.

CD Track List

1 Greetings in the Lulamoogi/Lugwere dialect of the Lutenga language of Busoga, eastern Uganda, "spoken" by members of the Bakuseka Majja Women's Group in Kibaale village, 1999. Used by permission of Centurio Balikoowa.

2 & 3 *Filulu* performance by Charles Bungu in Nyanhugi village, Sukumaland, Tanzania, 1999. Used by permission of Charles Bungu.

4 Excerpt of *Bugóbogóbo* by the Bana Sesilia Group of the Bujora Cultural Centre, Bujora, Tanzania, 1999. Used by permission of Charles Mahenda, Bujora Cultural Center.

5 "Muliranwa" ["My Neighbor"], *embaire* performance by the Ekidha Tobana Kabaliga Group in Bugwere village, Uganda 1999. Used by permission of Centurio Balikoowa.

6 Excerpt, *Chakacha*, performed by the Horizon Players Group and the Choir from the Muslim Secondary School, Kisumu, western Kenya. Used by permission of Lawrence Chiteri.

7 Excerpt illustrating the processional from the church at Bujora, Sukumaland, down the mountain to the Bulabo ceremonial stadium in Kisesa, 1999. Used by permission of Gregory Barz.

8 An example of *wigaashe* recorded at the Bulabo competition, 1999. Used by permission of Charles Mahenda, Bujora Cultural Center.

9 "Mahali ni Pazuri" ["This Place is Beautiful"], second verse, sung at a *Mashindano ya Kwaya* held at Kariakoo Lutheran Church in Dar es Salaam, 1993. Used by permission of Gideon Mdegella, Lutheran Choir Community Leader.

10 *Wimbo wa KiHehe*, a KiHehe melody, sung by the choir of the Mikocheni Anglican Church at a *Mashindano ya Kwaya* held at St. Alban's Anglican Church, Dar es Salaam, 1993. Used by permission of Gideon Mdegella, Lutheran Choir Community Leader.

11 "Sikieni Neno" ["Hear the Word"], a WaGogo melody, sung by the *Kwaya ya Vijana* of Kariakoo Lutheran Church, Dar es Salaam, 1993. Used by permission of Erneza Madeghe, Kariakoo, Lutheran church.

12 Author's interview with Gideon Mdegella, *mwalimu*, *Kwaya ya Upendo*, Azania Front Lutheran Cathedral, Dar es Salaam, 1994. Used by permission of Gideon Mdegella.

13 " 'Sikiliza,' Asema Bwana," Gideon Mdegella, composer and conductor, recording of a rehearsal of *Kwaya ya Upendo*, Azania Front Lutheran Cathedral, Dar es Salaam, 1994. Used by permission of Gideon Mdegella.

14 Tuning demonstration on the *endere* (flute), performed by Centurio Balikoowa, 1999. Used by permission of Centurio Balikoowa.

15 "Oo samba bambalele," a demonstration on the short *endere* (flute), performed by Centurio Balikoowa, 1999. Used by permission of Centurio Balikoowa.

16 Demonstration on the long *endere* (flute), performed by Centurio Balikoowa, 1999. Used by permission of Centurio Balikoowa.

17 Demonstration of the scale used on the *endingidi* (tubefiddle), performed by Centurio Balikoowa, 1999. Used by permission of Centurio Balikoowa.

18 *Endingidi* (tubefiddle) medley, performed by Centurio Balikoowa and Gregory Barz ("Adimudong'," "Twalamatagange," and a piece from the Central Region), 1999. Used by permission of Centurio Balikoowa and Gregory Barz.

19 Demonstration of elaboration on the *endingidi* (tubefiddle), performed by Centurio Balikoowa, 1999. Used by permission of Centurio Balikoowa.

20 Demonstration of the tuning of the *ntongooli* (bowl lyre), performed by Centurio Balikoowa, 1999. Used by permission of Centurio Balikoowa.

21 Demonstration of the *ntongooli* (bowl lyre), performed by Centurio Balikoowa, 1999. Used by permission of Centurio Balikoowa.

22 Demonstration of tuning of "Twalamatagange" on *ntongooli* (bowl lyre) and *endingidi*, performed by Centurio Balikoowa and Kiria Moses, 1999. Used by permission of Centurio Balikoowa.

23 Medley: Performance of the Ugandan National Anthem, "Oluyimba Lwe'eggwanga (Ebbona lya Afirika)" ["The Pearl of Africa"], the

Buganda Anthem, "Ekitiibwa kya Buganda" ["The Pride of Buganda"], and the Africa House Anthem, "Marching Along," performed by students at Makerere College School, 2002. Used by permission of Kitogo George Ndugwa, leader.

24 Demonstration of *endingidi* playing, performed by Kiria Moses, *endingidi* and voice, 1999. Used by permission of Centurio Balikoowa (for Kiria Moses).

25 Blair String Quartet demonstrates the timbre of *endingidi* in "Mu Kkubo Ery 'Omusaalaba." Used by permission of Mark Wait, Blair School of Music.

26 Demonstration of the *baakisimba* drum, the rhythm associated with *Baakisimba*, performed by Gregory Barz, 1999. Used by permission of Gregory Barz.

27 Blair String Quartet demonstrates the drumming in "Mu Kkubo Ery 'Omusaalaba." Used by permission of Mark Wait, Blair School of Music.

28 Demonstration of *Omunazi, Omwawuzi,* and *Omukonezi* parts played by Kiria Moses, Waiswa, and Centurio Balikoowa, 1999. Used by permission of Centurio Balikoowa (for himself, Waiswa, and Kiria Moses).

29 The Blair String Quartet demonstrates interlocking parts in "Mu Kkubo Ery 'Omusaalaba." Used by permission of Mark Wait, Blair School of Music.

30 Andericus Apondi, *nyatiti,* demonstrates the *Benga* guitar style on *nyatiti,* Kisumu, Kenya. Used by permission of Peter Nyamenya, Kisumu Museum, National Museums of Kenya.

31 "Jo Piny," performed by Kabila Klan, Kisumu, Kenya. Used by permission of Lawrence Oyuga, director.

32 "Kumbaya," performed by the congregation of the Power of Jesus Around the World Church, Kisumu, Kenya. Used by permission of Peter Nyamenya, Kisumu Museum, National Museums of Kenya.

33 Foreign terms introduced in this volume, pronounced by the author.

CHAPTER 1

Heating Up!

Haba na haba, hujaza kibaba
When combined, small things make up big things
[KiSwahili proverb printed on a woman's khanga cloth wrap]

EAST AFRICA

East Africa, often referred to as the "cradle of humanity," is the geographic home to the Great Rift Valley cutting through the center of this area of sub-Saharan Africa. The Rift Valley—the location for the famous archaeological digs at Olduvai Gorge in Tanzania and in areas surrounding Lake Turkana in Kenya by Louis and Mary Leakey—has produced human skulls that, once unearthed and analyzed, contributed to an estimate of life in this area dating back over 2.5 million years. East Africa is home to many peoples, representing all distinct language classificatory types known in Africa, although some are now isolated within a small area within the region. Bantu and Nilotic speakers comprise the majority of Africans in this area, but there are also several small but flourishing pockets of Cushitic speakers.

The countries comprising the area commonly referred to as East Africa include those in the "Horn," coastal, central, and southern areas—Burundi, Comoros Islands, Djibouti, Eritrea, Ethiopia, Kenya, Rwanda, Seychelles, Somalia, Tanzania, and Uganda, and including areas of Mozambique, Sudan, Zambia, and Malawi. For logistical reasons, this volume cannot provide a cohesive or detailed overview of the musical cultures of all East African countries; the rich diversity of traditions in this part of the world precludes an in-depth or comprehensive study of the entire geographic region. As a compromise, the musical contexts of three historically linked countries will be discussed—Kenya, Tanzania, and Uganda—in an attempt to approach the expressive culture of East Africa in a meaningful and historically logical way.

A highly developed system of trading networks penetrated East Africa historically for centuries, creating a system of cultural influences extending from as far east as the island of Zanzibar, linking across the Indian Ocean to India and beyond, as well as to areas deep within Central Africa. Spices, slaves, gold, and ivory were exported along these trading routes. Elsewhere, hunting, fishing, herding, and farming were historically the main contributors to local economies. In addition, many pastoralist and migratory patterns have occurred in East Africa over time—some voluntary, others forced. Colonial presence in the area began in the late sixteenth century with Portuguese forces that continued until 1720. Omani Arab control influenced coastal East Africa until Germany and Great Britain began their colonial rule in the nineteenth century. German colonial rule of present-day Tanzania ended after World War I when the League of Nations awarded mainland Tanzania—known then as Tanganyika—as a mandate to Britain (which already ruled Kenya and Uganda). The three countries achieved independence in the early 1960s: Tanzania (1961), Uganda (1962), and Kenya (1963). See Figure 1.1 for a map of East Africa.

Contemporary East Africa participates in the increasingly global economy of today's world. Cell phones have become ubiquitous in many cities and towns, and the presence of Internet cafes on many street corners greatly expands the geographic borders of Africa where Celine Dion, the Backstreet Boys, and Britney Spears dominate the airwaves. Traditional music performances throughout this region of the world, however, reflect both the peoples' participation in urban modernity and the maintenance of rural life for many peoples (see Chapter 5 of this volume for a more specific treatment of this idea).

A plurality of music-making styles and traditions exists within Kenya, Tanzania, and Uganda. Along the Indian Ocean mainland coast as well as in the coastal islands, *taarab* music is frequently performed, from the southern tip of Somalia down to the coast of Mozambique. *Taarab* (*Taarabu* in Swahili), a fusion of Arab and Indian melodies with rich, highly nuanced Swahili poetry is performed at weddings, at celebrations of rites of passage, and as an accompaniment for political issues and campaigns. In addition to *taarab*, choirs abound in East Africa. Many churches in East Africa support multiple choirs. Politicians and political parties rely on choirs to get their messages out to the people. Popular choirs entertain youth in multiple contexts. Next door to the churches, in small social clubs and larger hall venues, dance bands perform nightly to both large and small crowds in both rural and urban settings, playing a variety of musics ranging from Central African

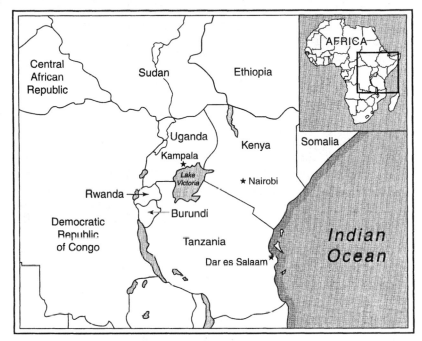

FIGURE 1.1 *Map of East Africa.*

Lingala dance music, covers of Western popular songs, and earlier local variants such as *benga* or *zilizopendwa*. Kiosks that sell cassette recordings litter the streets, markets, and bus depots of every town, large and small, offering local and foreign, popular and traditional musics for public consumption.

It is within this very active and vibrant everyday soundscape that both traditional music making and modern African musical genres are encouraged and supported (see Chapter 4). Despite the growing popularity of urban dance musics, performances of traditional music are still omnipresent in many rural areas, and they are now often taught in public schools in both urban and rural areas (see Chapters 2, 3, and 4). Drumming, singing, and dancing continue to function today as important means for mediating conflict, solidifying community and ethnicity, and educating in terms of "traditional" values and societal histories (see Chapter 2). The case studies, reflections, documentation, analyses, and interpretation of contemporary performances presented throughout this volume introduce ways of understanding musical change and adaptation in this greater cultural area that are in large part due to migration, colonization, missionization and the emergence of recent nationalistic and government interventions.

TRADITIONAL MUSIC PERFORMANCE: THE EXAMPLE OF *NGOMA*

The term *ngoma* is often used in this region of sub-saharan Africa in relation to music. While it is not used universally, it nevertheless seems to function for many as a cover term for "traditional music performance." You, too, might find it useful as a way to think about music in East Africa. *Ngoma*, a Bantu-derived term adopted into the KiSwahili language, is pronounced as "nn-**GÓH**-mah." (*Note*—a pronunciation guide for key terms introduced in this text is provided on CD track 33.)

As a typical *ngoma* performance takes awhile to attract and engage an audience fully, I now begin the process of "heating up" a discussion of *ngoma* by introducing two East African voices—Lawrence Chiteri and Ayisha Kyamugisha—as they respond to the question, "What does the term *ngoma* mean to you?"

Lawrence Chiteri—In Kenya the term *ngoma* could mean playing music that is dominated by drumming. On the other hand, around this side of Lake Victoria (gestures southwest toward Tanzania) they look at *ngoma* as anything that is danceable, any song that they could dance to, but whose main instrument is the drum. Whatever you sing, whatever you do where the instrumentation is dominated by drumming, that is *ngoma*. *We use the term ngoma only to refer to music.* Most people of Kenya talk of "I'm going to *ngoma*," and maybe they're only going to put on a cassette recorder . . . to them *ngoma* refers to any music, something that is musical and can be danced to. That is what we consider *ngoma*.

Ayisha Kyamugisha—*Ngoma* means "music" in some parts of Uganda. There is a similar word in Luganda, *abagoma*, meaning people who entertain other people. *Abagoma* refers to those people who perform for their daily food. They call music *ngoma* in the western part of the country [Uganda] as well.

The coupling of *ngoma* with drumming and dancing is at the heart of this term's meaning as a performance of traditional music in East

Africa as ethnomusicologist Peter Cooke points out in the *"Ngoma"* entry in *The New Grove Dictionary of Music and Musicians* (2000, xvii:855–56):

> *Ngoma* [is a] common term (with many variants) used generically for many kinds of drum among the numerous Bantu-speaking peoples of central, eastern-central and southern Africa. However, "ngoma" often has a wider meaning, at its widest standing for music and dancing (and the associated feasting), and for ceremonies in which drumming occurs. . . . Among different peoples *ngoma* can variously denote a dance, a drum ensemble, the most important drum of an ensemble, or individual drums. Use of the name is sometimes indicative that drums have special sacred or magical properties.

The "wider meaning" of this term outlined by Peter Cooke, then, resonates with the thinking of Lawrence Chiteri, a director of a troupe that specializes in the performance of *ngoma* in the country of Kenya. For Chiteri, the term refers to both something specific—that is, music intended for dancing that is accompanied by drumming—and something general—such as a cover term for "music." For Ayisha Kyamugisha, a dancer and trainer with a *ngoma* troupe in Uganda, the term is inextricably linked with the English-language term, "music."

WHAT IS "MUSIC" IN EAST AFRICA?

> In traditional African societies, music making is generally organized as a social event. Public performances, therefore, take place on social occasions—that is, occasions when members of a group or a community come together for the enjoyment of leisure, for recreational activities, or for the performance of a rite, ceremony, festival, or any kind of collective activity, such as building bridges, clearing paths, going on a search party, or putting out fires—activities that, in industrialized societies, might be assigned to specialized agencies. (J. H. Kwabena Nketia, *The Music of Africa*, 1974:21)

For many East Africans, the concept of "music" does not exist, at least not in the sense we may be most familiar with. In many studies of East Africa, the line between what is music and what is not music often blurs, especially as "musical" elements in everyday life are heard and experienced. A pertinent example of this is the highly stylized form of greetings detailed in the following fieldnote excerpt, typical of the author's experiences in small Ugandan villages (CD track 1). This example is decidedly *not* "music" per se, but rather a highly stylized form

FIGURE 1.2 *The author recording three women exchanging greetings in Kibaale-Busiki village under a hastily built tarpaulin. Virimiina Nakiranda faces the camera wearing a necklace. The women all wear traditional Eastern Ugandan dress. Notice the* likembe—*plucked lamellaphones—that surround the women on the ground. (Photo by Centurio Balikoowa.)*

of greeting. This example is included to allow a stretching of our meaning of "music" to embrace expressive aspects of language as "musical."

Excerpt from Fieldnotes. *During a break in a recording session in the remote village of Kibaale-Busiki (Busoga, Eastern Uganda), caused by downpour of heavy rains, I retreat for cover under a makeshift tarpaulin along with a group of performers from the Bakuseka Majja Women's Group (see Figure 1.2). As I begin to put my recording equipment away, my Ugandan research colleague, Centurio Balikoowa, stops me, pointing to a woman approaching us. "You must continue recording, you must document this." He continued proudly, "Our greetings in Busoga are the longest in*

Uganda.*" As I set up my microphones he smiles as he continues, "Now you will hear some real music!" With my microphones back on their stands Virimiina Nakiranda, the
leader of Bakuseka Majja along with another member greet
the approaching member as she enters the area under the
tarpaulin.*

ACTIVITY 1.3   *First, listen to CD track 1 all the way through
for the first time. The recorded excerpt is from the extended exchange of greetings referred to in the fieldnotes quoted above. Next,
listen to the recorded example all the way through for a second
time. Get the "sounds" of the exchange of greetings in your ear.
Listen again to CD track 1. This time refer to the melodic transcription provided in Figure 1.3. The melodic transcription attempts to graph several of the more evident "sounds," allowing
them to become transformed into and perceived as "musical" aspects of the exchange. Figure 1.3 is not provided as a musical
transcription of the event; rather it is intended as a musical map,
one that demonstrates movement between several important pitch
or tonal centers.*

- Do you *hear* the exchange any differently the second time
  you listen to it?
- Do you *hear* the exchange any differently after consulting the
  transcription?

As you listen a third time you might be able to follow the English
translation of the excerpt provided next. The women who are greeting
each other are Virimiina Nakiranda (leader) and two other members of
the Bakuseka Majja Women's Group, Kibaale-Busiki (Busoga, Uganda).
The specific greetings presented in CD track 1 are in the Lulamoogi/
Lugwere dialect of the Lutenga language of Busoga, eastern Uganda.

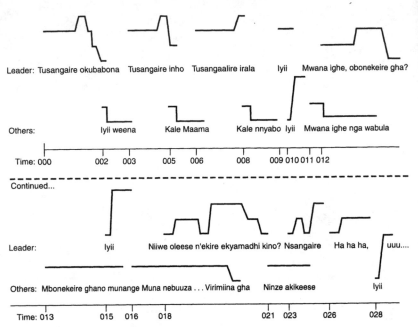

FIGURE 1.3 *Musical map of the greetings in the Lulamoogi/Lugwere dialect of the Lutenga language of Busoga, eastern Uganda, "spoken" by members of the Bakuseka Majja Women's Group in Kibaale village.*

GREETINGS (EXCERPT)

Tusangaire okubabona / Iyii weena / Tusangaire inho / Kale Maama / Tusangaire inho / Kale nnyabo / Tusangaalire irala / Kale nnyabo / Iyii / Mwana ighe nga wabula / Mwana ighe, obonekeire gha? / Mbonekeire ghano munange / Iyii / Muna nebuuza nti Virimiina yabulira gha / niiwe oleese n'ekire ekyamadhi kino? / Ninze akikeese / Iyii / Nsangiare / Ha ha ha, uuuu. . . . / Webale okughaya nabageni / Iyii / Webale inho / Tuli kughaya nabo mpola-mpola / Mweena mwebale kwiidha kumbeeresaku bageni bano / Omughala ighe! / Kino kinene / Nnnn? / Wabulira gha? / Eyo mu Kibaale aye muna endhala yaluma ife yatumalamu / Muna tweena n'ebugweeri eyo n'ebutembe n'eluwuka / Yoona kyatuuka yo / Byona-Byoona / Iiii, banange. . . . / Ife twatendukirangamuku agho nobweerere / Tulobe kuba abaise Musobya / Aye omwise Musobya atughe kuliina tumanhe eriina tweena tweyagale / Nabageni bano / Tumugheku n'akemba tumughemuku nakazira / Akoze bulungi, ha ha ha, uuuu

We are happy to see you / Yes, you too / We are so happy / OK, Mama / We are so happy / OK, madam / We are happy indeed / OK, madam / Eeee / Child, you are lost / You, where do you come from? / I come from here, my friend / Eeee / Friend, I've been asking myself were you, Virimiina, were you the one who brought this rain cloud? / I am the one who has brought it / Eeee / I am happy / Ha ha ha, uuuu. . . . / Thank you for conversing with the visitors / Eeee / Thank you so much / We are conversing with them slowly / You too, thank you for coming to assist me with the visitors / But friend, we are happy for the visitors / You go girl! / This is marvelous / What? / Where have you been hiding? / There in Kibaale friend, famine has drained all our strength / Friend, we too in Bugwere, there even in Butembe, Luwuka / There too it reached / All the villages / Oh, friends. . . . / We sometimes slept without a meal, with nothing / If we didn't have the members of the Musobya clan / But the members of Musobya gave us the name so that we can / know it and also be glad / With these visitors / We will sing a song and give him ululations / He has done well, ha ha ha, uuuu

As you read through the text of the greetings the performance may very well return in your mind to a linguistic exchange. Such stylized greetings occur in many parts of Africa, and local peoples often do not regard these exchanges as specifically musical. Yet, the heightened forms of communication point to musical properties that exist in many African languages, and at several levels these exchanges involve interaction between local rhythms, linguistic tones, and phonological sound structures. What "we" may perceive as music is often in fact a deeply rooted exchange of cultural greetings, an establishment of human relationships within an African context.

Shifting south now from Uganda to Sukumaland in Tanzania, no one would find the designation of *filulu* (flute) music as "music" to be an unfamiliar one.

Excerpt from Fieldnotes. *As I make the steep climb up the mountain from Kisesa to Nyanhugi village in Sukumaland, Tanzania, I pass several groups of women singing as they use their hoes in an attempt to dig areas for planting in the extremely parched dry earth. Pausing to rest in a shaded area along the pathway, I hear the sound of a lone flute player slowly approaching me on the footpath. Before long, a man*

comes up behind me, introducing himself as Charles Bungu,
a driver for the local pastor. In an exchange in the KiSwahili
language, I compliment him on his flute playing. He thanks
me, and offers to sing another song for me and for the work-
ing women on his filulu, *a small, two-hole aerophone. Af-*
ter thanking him for agreeing to "play" a piece for me, Charles
smiles and tells me that rather than play he will now "sing"
for me on his filulu.

A few days after first meeting Charles Bungu, a driver for the village priest in Nyanhugi, he was recorded "singing" two different pieces on two different *filulu* (CD track 2 and CD track 3). Bungu made each of the *filulu* that he plays in these examples by and for himself (this is typical—a *filulu* player makes his or her own instrument).

A typical *filulu* flute is a made from the naturally hollow end of the tailpiece of a dried calabash (long-neck dipper gourd), which is then stopped by two end pieces that then have holes drilled into them. The hand drilling of a mouth hole completes the making of the *filulu*. Each end piece is then stopped or opened at both ends by the player's thumbs in performance in order to produce different pitches. Each instrument is unique, creating variances in pitch and tone color due to the individual calabash and thickness of the *filulu*, and the positions of the holes that are drilled into them (see Figure 1.4). There is no need to match pitches on this instrument with any other, since the *filulu* is invariably played alone for one's own enjoyment. As you listen to CD tracks 2 and 3 you should note that five distinct pitches are produced on each *filulu*; on CD track 2 the four main pitches are particularly clear.

- Blowing into the mouth hole with the ends unstopped produces the first pitch
- Closing one end hole with a thumb generates a second pitch
- Closing the other end hole with a thumb makes a third pitch
- Stopping both end holes with both thumbs produces a fourth pitch
- Overblowing creates a fifth and final pitch, that is blowing hard with both end holes stopped

CD track 2 begins with a repeated opening gesture. Through this the performer gives voice to the name of the instrument, the *filulu*, as he

FIGURE 1.4   *Close-up of two* filulu.   *(Photo by Jonathan Rogers.)*

plays four distinct notes—"fi," "lu-uu," and "lu." In Figure 1.5, a brief melodic transcription, you will find a graph that introduces the opening melodic gesture that is repeated four times. *Note*: only four of the possible five pitches are played in this selection, and these pitches have been placed in the four spaces between five lines. The highest pitch is stressed in Bungu's playing, indicating that it is a structural note, and this is indicated in the transcription (as is the final note in the repeated, melodic gesture to a lesser extent). Other notes, marked with "Xs," sound almost as if they are intended as ornamental or passing notes.

CD track 3 is played on the second *filulu* to the right in Figure 1.4. You will quickly notice a distinct change in timbre and pitch between the two *filulu* played in CD track 2 and CD track 3. Bungu begins the second recording with the same opening melodic gesture—singing "*filulu*"—but beyond that he offers a much more detailed, more nuanced performance.

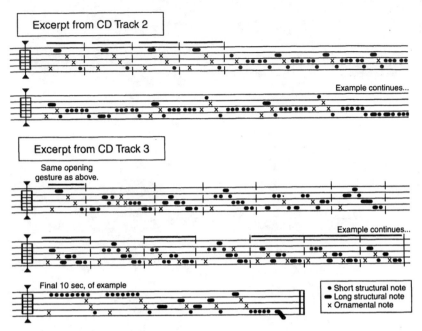

FIGURE 1.5 *Melodic transcription of* Filulu *pattern.*

ACTIVITY 1.2 *The melodic transcriptions provided here are of excerpts of these two examples and are intended to indicate two things: pitch and duration of the notes played in each example. The symbols used are meant to indicate duration and stress, that is, the length Bungu remains on each pitch he plays. Variance in pitch is indicated by the four spaces between the five lines.*

- Follow this melodic transcription as you listen to CD track 2 and CD track 3, and then decide for yourself whether such a graphing of musical sound communicates or indicates something significant to you within these two performances.

- Next, create a chart or diagram that communicates *your* understanding of the two performances.

• Consider whether such charts and diagrams help you "hear" the melodic inventiveness of Charles Bungu's playing any differently.

The *filulu* is a musical instrument of the Sukuma people who live in an area in northwest Tanzania (see Figure 1.1, map). According to Bungu, the *filulu* evokes the sounds of birds found in Sukumaland, and he often mimics birdcalls with his melodic gestures, and this is perhaps why he referred to his playing as singing.

There are many centers of similar and varying cultural practices in Sukumaland, home for over 5 million Sukuma people, the largest ethnic group in Tanzania. Many Sukuma, however, still live in rural villages. Farming is a collective or family activity for the Sukuma people who are also known as cattle herders. A growing number of Sukuma have begun moving to urban centers, where different cultures and multiethnic influences affect Sukuma expressive culture.

If the term "music" does exist in Sukumaland or in other areas of East Africa it is usually conceptualized within a wider set of parameters. Frequently a foreign term has been introduced to local languages, such as *muziki* in KiSwahili, but such terms often refer specifically to Western-influenced musical performance, not to localized, traditional music performances. Thus, throughout this text local, indigenous East African concepts are utilized for understanding musical phenomena. In any case, "music" in most East Africans' lives is not set aside as an object to be studied or examined.

By extension, music is typically not *transcribed, notated,* or *analyzed* in the stylized ways presented in this volume. Music *is,* however, often recorded, traded, sold, practiced, performed, and discussed. It is purposefully woven into the fabric of everyday life and reflected on from the moment one wakes until one falls asleep listening to the sounds of a neighboring village's *embaire* (xylophone) ensemble as it plays through the night in eastern Uganda, for instance.

Throughout this text local ways of knowing and understanding music in East Africa will be approached (such as the earlier *ngoma* example) specifically within an interactive performance of both tradition and modernity. Contemporary traditional performances often include, for instance, the origins of the local tradition itself, elaborating musically on how the tradition began, who was instrumental in developing it, and who has maintained it. Among the Baganda people in central Uganda (Buganda), for example, a traditional dance that originated many years ago in the royal Baganda court is performed called *Baakisimba*. *Baakisimba* demonstrates how history and cultural context are often interactive and reenacted within contemporary performance. Most, if not all, traditional dances in East Africa have similar, deep histories supporting their performances. The *Baakisimba* dance music was "invented" in response to the *kabaka* (king) of Buganda who became "happy" one day after drinking some local brew made from ripe bananas. "You know, we're not supposed to say that the *kabaka* is drunk in Uganda; we say the *kabaka* is happy," according to Ugandan musician Centurio Balikoowa. After drinking the local brew, the *kabaka* began to weave around the palace as he walked, and the story goes that the people who lived in the palace looked at him and thought, "Well, if the *kabaka* is walking like that, then shouldn't we do the same?" And they began to mimic the "happy" *kabaka's* walk. When they followed the *kabaka*, the women began to imitate his inebriated gestures by slowly shaking their buttocks. The men went to the drums and started to play a rhythm that directly imitated the *kabaka's* walk. *Baakisimba* literally means "those who planted it," referring to the planting of the banana trees from which the *kabaka's* happy local brew was made. Today there are two forms of *Baakisimba*, one for the *kabaka* and one for the people. Yet, in both forms dancers (both male and female) continue to dance with their feet always close to the ground in order to avoid kicking dust up in the air in front of the King (whether or not present).

CONCLUSION

As you continue to work your way through this volume, take notice of the various roles an expanded notion of music is capable of adopting in the everyday lives of East Africans. Identify the different ways traditional music is maintained, adapted, and contextualized in different East African communities. In Chapter 2 the social contexts of traditional music and dance widespread throughout East Africa are outlined in greater detail with the aid of several case studies that support the argument that music and dance participate with multiple worlds—historical and contemporary. Chapter 3 includes several examples of ways in which very different forms of musical competitions project a variety of social identities. There are many levels of competition in everyday life in East Africa, and several examples are presented that challenge the historically important role of music in negotiating historical continuity as well as modernity. Chapter 4 introduces issues related to the musical careers of two important East African musicians—Gideon Mdegella of Tanzania and Centurio Balikoowa of Uganda—both of whom live in multiple musical worlds and communicate in multiple musical languages. Finally, in Chapter 5 issues are presented concerning how traditional musical materials are infused within new musical forms as well as reinvented traditions for many popular and art traditions in East Africa. In the conclusion to this volume several ways are suggested to reflect on the role of music in the performance of tradition and modernity in East Africa, that is the power of music to function as a means of communication for communities to themselves, to neighbors (close and regional), and to the outside world.

CHAPTER 2

Traditional Performances in Two Villages and a Town

> *East Africa is really one large village.*
> *And this village celebrates with so many different musics.*
> —Sam Okello, Ndere Troupe (Kampala, Uganda)

INTRODUCTION

To demonstrate the multivalent nature and functions of *traditional performances* as rooted within musical and social systems that in many ways unify much if not all of East Africa, three case studies are offered in this chapter. Each case study introduces a specific cultural context and musical characteristic of traditional music performance in Tanzania, Uganda, and Kenya—within two villages and a town. Additionally, each case study contributes to a framework within which *traditional music performance* as an event, as a principle, and as an institution can be understood.

> *Event*—The case studies support an understanding of traditional music performances as events that are planned, rehearsed, and celebrated, and that transmit important aspects of culture from one generation to the next.
>
> *Principle*—The case studies also demonstrate a basic principle of traditional music performance, that is community formation, reflecting the varying ways traditional music performance is understood, used, and embraced in East Africa to express both interdependence and integration within communities.
>
> *Institution*—Finally, the case studies also document particular ways in which traditional music performances aid in establishing and solidifying social institutions that not only define communities but also distinguish internal differences within communities.

The case studies introduced in this chapter—*Bugóbogóbo*, *"Muliranwi,"* and *Chakacha*—provide a general overview of several very different ways traditional music performances function in very different Tanzanian, Ugandan, and Kenyan communities in East Africa. As outlined in the first chapter, these examples serve three fundamental purposes—each marks off time within the context of a special event, each represents the principle of integration and interdependence, and each demonstrates a position within deeply rooted cultural institutions. Some of the many ancillary roles and functions of traditional music performances that are highlighted in these case studies can be summarized in the following ways.

Bugóbogóbo

• In the performance of *Bugóbogóbo*, it is clear that a primary function is to contribute to the goals of community formation and solidification among the Sukuma people of Tanzania.

• Traditional music performances often communicate what it means to be part of a particular "tribe," an "ethnic group," or an individual "clan." *Bugóbogóbo* communicates what it means to be Sukuma both to the Sukuma people and to others (non-Sukuma).

• Specific forms of music that incorporate dance, such as *Bugóbogóbo*, are used as badges of communal individuality for voluntary associations and social indemnity groups, that is groups organized to aid in and facilitate the social needs of a community.

"Muliranwi"

• Traditional music performances bring individuals together and hold them together, by communicating and affirming communally held morals and values as demonstrated by this Ugandan community.

Chakacha

• In addition to projecting localized identities, traditional music performances may just as often communicate a pan-ethnic identity. For example, when performing music-dances such as *Chakacha*, young Luo women communicate not only what it means to be from western Kenya, but also what it is to be Kenyan in general.

The case studies that follow outline unique positions assumed by traditional musical performances in this region of Africa, while demonstrating both the deep roots and broad and popular appeal of such music among several different peoples. Each study is framed with personal fieldnotes composed as reflections on the author's field research within East African communities. The opening fieldnotes are intended not only to evoke a setting—to set the stage, if you will—but also to provide critical details concerning the individual cultural contexts.

CASE STUDY #1: NYANHUGI VILLAGE, SUKUMALAND, TANZANIA

While traditional music performances occur throughout the year in Sukumaland, competitions following the harvest seasons in many villages are now dominant sites for public music performance and popular entertainment. (See Chapter 3 for an elaboration of another site—the competition.) In the fieldnote on the approach to Nyanhugi Village presented earlier, it is noted the groups of women hoeing to dig areas for planting. The hoe—typically used in everyday farming—is an important symbol among the Sukuma people (Figure 2.1). *Igembe* hoes are fea-

FIGURE 2.1 *The* igembe *hoe is used throughout Sukumaland, Tanzania. As discussed in the following passages, the* igembe *is a symbol used to communicate "Sukuma-ness" to both Sukuma and non-Sukuma in the Bugóbogóbo ngoma. (Photo by Gregory Barz.)*

tured in several dances and music making in general, and typically relate music to aspects of Sukuma agriculture and labor, such as in the famous *Bugóbogóbo* dance music. While living in Nyanhugi Village, Mzee Kang'wina—a local Sukuma elder—assigned the author a Sukuma name, Ligembe, referring not directly to the *igembe* hoe, but rather indirectly to the ethnomusicologist's insistence on "digging" for answers to many questions. Now, more about *Bugóbogóbo*.

Excerpt from Fieldnotes. *The dancers at the Kisesa Stadium in Sukumaland (Tanzania) dramatically dropped their hoes on the ground and a cloud of dust quickly enveloped the performance area signaling the end of a performance segment of Bugóbogóbo. Several of the older dancers ran over to a large wooden box and quickly pulled out four rather large snakes. Wrapping them around their bodies, they run through the crowd. The snakes were a big hit among the children as the dancers very deliberately began performing with the snakes, occasionally placing the snakes' heads in their mouths to the squeals of many. The children kept running away screaming whenever a dancer approached with a snake. They, of course, would creep back up in curiosity. There was not much actual "dancing" with the snakes. As the dancers picked up their hoes once more and finished performing the Bugóbogóbo segment, another group on the other side of the arena began to attract people away as they began performing the famous porcupine dance called Banungule.*

Bugóbogóbo is a traditional *mbiina* (or *ngoma*)—or "music-dance" as outlined in the first chapter—that often serves a specific function in Sukuma culture. Principally, it facilitates work; labor is made easier, for example, when performing *Bugóbogóbo* (CD track 4). As ethnomusicologist Frank Gunderson suggests, Sukuma musical performances such as *Bugóbogóbo* contribute in the following five ways to a successful work atmosphere:

- First, music at the labor site creates a desire to work, and to work together with others, thus creating good values in impressionable youth.

- Second, music at the labor site provides one with the ability to work longer hours without being tired.

- Third, music at the labor site calms its listeners and focuses their mental energies and organizational skills.

- Fourth, music at the labor site creates joy in the worker, casting off worries and suffering.

- Fifth and finally, songs at the work site contain important life testimonies and teaching and are enthusiastically and vividly received as such.

Performances of tradition music—such as *Bugóbogóbo*—function in different ways within different Sukuma communities, yet a primary feature of the *Bugóbogóbo* performance remains its ability to signal to the community and to the outside world what it means to be "Sukuma." It also clearly demonstrates the interdependence of drumming, singing, and dancing, and their inseparability from everyday life. According to Gunderson, *Bugóbogóbo* became a presentational form in the late 1920s when *bagóbogóbo* farmer's dance-labor groups in Sukumaland were formed. The *bagóbogóbo*—which means "wearers of animal skins"— were so named because the farmer-performer—who carried *igembe* hoes—typically wore the skins of leopards, jackals, and hyenas, in addition to ostrich feathers and porcupine quills. Bells were also attached to the dancers' hoe handles so that the hoes would produce additional, complementary rhythms.

I first witnessed a performance of *Bugóbogóbo* in the early 1990s outside of Sukumaland in a small social club in Dar es Salaam, a major city along the Indian Ocean coast of Tanzania. An out-of-town touring music and dance ensemble that specialized in a diverse repertoire of traditional musics offered the performance. The assembled crowd's reaction to the ensemble was enthusiastic as the dancers returned to the performance venue with hoes in hand, immediately signaling for many the highly athletic *Bugóbogóbo*. A brilliantly choreographed version of *Bugóbogóbo* ensued; it was later confirmed that none of the performers in the troupe were themselves Sukuma, a fact that concerned the audience to no great degree. For many audiences (and for performers) throughout the country, *Bugóbogóbo* has become a Sukuma contribution to and symbol of Tanzanian national identity. It has even become popular beyond Tanzania, in East Africa in general. A poster advertising a festival of traditional music and dance held in Kampala, Uganda, recently announced the arrival of Tanzanian "Snake Dancers" from

Sukumaland. It is interesting to note that the national identity in the case of the Ugandan poster assumed priority over the regional identity, that is the dancers were referred to as "Tanzanian from Sukumaland" not "Sukuma from Tanzania." The ability of *Bugóbogóbo* to communicate "Tanzanian" national identity rather than Sukuma regional identity is far-reaching within this area of the world.

On CD track 4 you will hear the youth group of the Bana Sesilia, affiliated with the Bujora Cultural Centre in the Tanzanian village of Nyanhugi, perform their version of *Bugóbogóbo* in a competition setting. The performance of *Bugóbogóbo* included in this volume was recorded during *Bulabo*, an extended post-harvest festival that celebrates the Roman Catholic feast of Corpus Christi throughout Sukumaland. This performance included elaborate hoe maneuvers reminiscent of military drills; such maneuvers have become typical for performances of *Bugóbogóbo*.

The selection begins with a *call-and-response* section—the leader issues a *"call"* as he arranges the seated dancers in four straight lines. He carries a flywhisk made from wildebeest tail hair, which he uses to gesture toward particular dancers. The dancers (both male and female) *"respond"* to the leader's call, singing in harmony, while the ensemble's drummers begin to provide rhythms by hitting their sticks against the sides of the drums, establishing a steady, fast pulse. The dancers quickly join in this rhythmic section by clapping along on every other pulse (elementary pulsation), the central beat of the repeating rhythmic cycle. Once the leader is satisfied with the arrangement of the dancers he approaches the drummers and gives them the signal to start. On cue, two male drummers playing large drums begin the rhythm outlined in Figure 2.2, based on a repeated *time cycle* that identifies *Bugóbogóbo*. The drum-cue can be heard clearly at 0:38 on CD track 4.

The leader gives a signal to the dancers—an indication that they should all rise from the ground—by blowing on a *filimbi* (whistle), which he carries around his neck. You can hear the leader's initial whistle signal warning on CD track 4 at 1:00 and more clearly at 1:18.

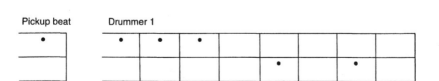

FIGURE 2.2 *Drum-cue in* Bugóbogóbo *ngoma.*

FIGURE 2.3   *Members of the Bana Sesilia Youth Group of the Bujora Cultural Centre in Nyanhugi village, Sukumaland, Tanzania, rehearse* Bugóbogóbo, *a* Sukuma *ngoma. Here the dancers mimic farming with their* igembe *(hoes). The leader blows on his whistle.   (Photo by Gregory Barz.)*

The dancers rise up and either squat on their heels or their knees as they continue to sing. In response to a subsequent *filimbi* signal all the dancers stand and begin to swing their arms back and forth as they step in place, keeping time along with the *Bugóbogóbo* rhythm. The women all wear matching *khangas* (elaborate, printed cloth with brief aphorisms or proverbs in KiSwahili whose meanings are typically multilayered, such as "*Haba na haba, hujaza kibaba*"—the proverb used to open this volume—wrapped around their waists (see Figure 2.3).

The leader begins whistling along on his *filimbi* as he dances, indicating that more elaborate dancing should begin. At one point he interjects the basic rhythmic figure in Figure 2.2 to indicate that men should start moving in one way as the women begin to move in another. This whistle signal warning can be distinctly heard on CD track 4 at 1:27.

After a brief period of dancing, the leader projects two long tones on his *filimbi* indicating to all that the dancing is to stop momentarily (at

1:54); in response the dancers all sit back down on the ground. Almost immediately the drummers commence a more energetic rhythm (at 1:56) while the dancers pick up their *igembe* (hoes) that have been on the ground next to them all the while. The dancers begin by dancing in place, twirling their *igembe* in front of them as they dance back and forth on their feet from heel to toe. On a cue from the leader, they begin to swing their short *igembe* around their necks and legs.

The dancers simultaneously drop their *igembe* hoes to the ground as they begin to rotate their shoulders in a continuous, rolling fashion. They pick up their *igembe* once more for a final routine, twirling the farming tools with great speed around their bodies; all movements in the music and dance are synchronized. Toward the end, the dancers mimic the motions of toiling the ground, spreading seeds, and hoeing the earth (see Figure 2.4).

The performance of *Bugóbogóbo* comes to a dramatic climax as several women, observers in the gathered crowd, begin to ululate—a high

FIGURE 2.4 *Members of the Bana Sesilia Group performing* Bugóbogóbo *during a festival competition in Kisesa village, Sukumaland, Tanzania. This particular festival attracts visitors from as far away as Denmark (and Nashville, Tennessee!). (Photo by Gregory Barz.)*

vocal cry interrupted by rapid movement of the tongue—to congratulate and praise the group for their performance. Such ululation is typically only executed by women and is widespread in East Africa, as well as in the Middle East and North Africa.

Very often rhythm—such as the rhythm associated with *Bugóbogóbo*—is conceptualized in African contexts as more complicated, more complex than rhythm is typically treated or understood in many Western musics. This may very well be an obvious truism, but for many of us it is a concept that bears exploring. For example, Western rhythms are, according to Ugandan musician Centurio Balikoowa, "straight," whereas East African rhythms often reflect and communicate something of the area from which they come. East African rhythms (as is true elsewhere in Africa) are in Balikoowa's understanding, more "complex" because they are performed by different ethnic groups who play assorted types of traditional music and who themselves maintain a variety of individual types of rhythms in their musical repertoires—musical or rhythmic difference is a critical factor for communicating, for example, Sukuma-ness. Many East African communities do not restrict themselves to performing one rhythm, however. As the *Bugóbogóbo* example demonstrates, multiple rhythmic patterns can and most often are embraced with a given *ngoma* or music dance.

Rhythm and music in general are integral aspects of everyday Sukuma life, and traditional music performances such as *Bugóbogóbo* emerge from and reference farming life, demonstrating the integration of labor and music in this area of Tanzania. Songs and the performance of specific traditional music dances occur during daily farm routines as well as during the post-harvest competition season. In addition to fulfilling spiritual, communal, and entertainment roles, performing *Bugóbogóbo* is also a primary means of regenerating or passing along Sukuma culture. *Bugóbogóbo* is so closely associated with what it means to be Sukuma that many aspects do not need to be "taught" since children have often been imitating their elders from a very early age. In Figure 2.5 a group of young children "perform" the intricate rhythmic patterns that accompany *Bugóbogóbo* in Sukumaland discussed earlier in this chapter. The empty Zesta jam tin cans and the rough wooden sticks used by the children allow them to be active receivers of local, traditional culture. Children in East Africa (as in other parts of Africa and the rest of the world) are often present whenever performances such as *Bugóbogóbo* occur, and they are often active participants in the transmission of traditional culture through their very presence.

FIGURE 2.5 *Young children in Nyanhugi village "accompany" the preparations for a* Bugóbogóbo ngoma *competition in Sukumaland.* (Photo by Gregory Barz.)

CASE STUDY #2: BUGWERE VILLAGE, BUSOGA REGION, EASTERN UGANDA

Excerpt from Fieldnotes. *A long drought is coming to an end, and these days there is not much reason for celebration in the Busoga region of Eastern Uganda. After a day of traveling on a series of buses from Kampala to Jinja—crossing the source of the Nile—and on to Iganga town, we arrange for another small bus to take us further inland. Finally, Centurio Balikoowa and I hop on the back of small mopeds and are driven along a series of narrow footpaths for the twenty-minute ride to Bugwere village. This is as remote a location as I have ever experienced. Along the way we pass huts made from sticks and mud clustered in family compounds. Small children come out to greet us as we sputter by. Approaching Bugwere village, people began gesturing, pointing us to our*

destination (Figure 2.6). When we stop, Mzee Rasidi Bidha Mpola, head of the family compound and leader of a local Bugwere village embaire (xylophone) performing group, greets us. Soon after we arrive, a seven-foot long, three and one-half-foot deep trench is dug in the center of the compound. Two large banana trees are cut and then laid down on either side of the trench to provide a frame onto which will be laid the wooden embaire keys. Over these two stalks are placed bundles of elephant grass wrapped in banana leaves, providing a resonant buffer between the wood keys and the banana stalks. Once the large keys are placed across the stalks it becomes apparent that the long trench will function as a resonating chamber. Several men of the village sit down around the embaire. Other men begin to wrap themselves in their dance attire. As the deep-toned embaire keys are first struck, the music resounds from one village to another, reverberating in the night air, and calling local villagers to gather.

FIGURE 2.6 *The pathway leading to Mzee Rasidi's family compound in Bugwere Village, Busoga, Uganda.* (Photo by Gregory Barz.)

"Is your tape recorder running? Quick, watch their hands! They're not using sticks! They're playing the *embaire* as if it was a drum," my Ugandan colleague Centurio Balikoowa shouted in my ear soon after we arrived in Bugwere village. Balikoowa, one of the best-known traditional musicians in the Busoga region of Eastern Uganda invited me to Bugwere to document an unprecedented moment of change and adaptation in his musical culture. At that moment the village was immediately enveloped by a complete transformation of the everyday soundscape in response to the sound of the hands beating on the lower *embaire* keys. This particular performance led by Ekidha Tobana Kabaliga—the village *embaire* (xylophone) ensemble—began in the early evening as farmers return from working in the fields. *Embaire* is a musical performance tradition that has historically included up to five instrumentalists, each of whom assumes a prescribed role to play on a large wooden-slat xylophone; others involved in the music making play *ngoma* (drums), *endingidi* (bowed tubefiddles), while still others function off to the side of the performance area as singers, chorus, and dancers.

As you listen to CD track 5, a performance of "Muliranwa" ["My Neighbor"], you will hear an assortment of instruments, including a *nsase* gourd shaker, a metal beater, a one-string, bowed *endingidi*, the large 21-key wooden *embaire*, as well as a solo singer and chorus. The opening section of the recording includes a wonderful demonstration of the importance of polyrhythms in this area of Africa, as different instruments punctuate and mark different cross rhythms.

The male vocal leader, known as the *omulesi owolwemba* ["the one who starts the song"], introduces the text as the chorus, collectively known as the *abanukuzi*, responds with a repetitive melodic line. The *omulesi owolwembu* and *abanukuzi* continue to develop and expand on this leader-chorus relationship throughout the performance.

omulesi owolwemba	lead, solo singer
abanukuzi	chorus

There is a distinct rhythmic break at 3:33 during the recording on CD track 5 as Mzee Rasidi, the person in charge of the *embaire* group, punctuates the *okwetegeka* rhythm—a rhythmic signal for the dancers to begin—on the high keys of the *embaire*. The *embaire* players begin to *dbuti* [clap with sticks] at this point while bystanders contribute an *obwara*, a repetitive, rhythmic clapping pattern. At 4:47 the leader beats out a rhythmic *mulindimuko* signal on the *embaire*, indicating to all the performers that the tempo should speed up and that the intensity of the dancing should also increase. A few seconds later the *embaire* leader finally gives the specific *okuwoya* rhythmic signal at 5:01 to indicate the beginning of an intensified rhythmic section that will bring the performance to an end. The signal is accompanied by the *omulesi owolwemba* shouting out, "*tamenaibuga nalufuka irongo*" [literally, "don't break the gourd"], indicating to all involved in the *embaire* performance that they should end this abbreviated performance.

There are dramatic variations of dynamics, tempo, and intensity throughout the performance of "Muliranwa," and the shifts between softer and louder sections indicate the importance of timbre as a compositional element in the traditional music of this region of East Africa. Most striking about this performance, however, is the group's significant addition of several large wooden keys placed at the lower end of the *embaire*. Each of these lower keys is played by an individual player and played more like drums (see later section).

The performance ends with a unique *okumala olwemba* played on the *embaire*. The *okumala olwemba* is a distinctive melodic gesture used to indicate closure in a performance. It is played on the *embaire*. Such signature endings are particular to individual groups, and they are designed to identify the performing group (although several local groups are known to share *okumala olwemba*); each group has a unique melodic pattern, a gesture used to signal closure. The *okumala olwemba* also helps the large group stop together. You can hear the Ekidha Tobana Kabaliga village ensemble's distinctive closing *okumala olwemba* begin at 5:16 in the last few seconds of "Muliranwa" on CD track 5. Ekidha Tobana Kabaliga's signature *okumala olwemba* is a melodic gesture that is repeated at the end of nearly every piece this group performs.

In Figure 2.7, the *okumala olwemba* performed on CD track 5 is transcribed according to the pitch names typically associated with the pentatonic, five-note tuning system used in many Ugandan cultures. The solmization or solfege syllables selected—Do, Re, Mi, La, and Sol—are the five syllables used by the Ekidha Tobana Kabaliga group. (The author remembers his Ugandan colleague, Centurio Balikoowa marking these very same solmization syllables with chalk on his *embaire* when he first learned to play the instrument.) The boxes in Figure 2.7 represent the lowest five keys on the *embaire*. The two lowest notes of the five indicated have been added and exist outside the beginning of the five-note scale pattern. Note that the semitone intervals—Ti–Do and Mi–Fa—do not occur on the *embaire* as melodic notes. They do however, occur as passing notes by the singer and other instrumentalists.

Sol	La	Do	Re	Mi

Lowest keys on the *Embaire*

Pitch string of the *Okumala Olwemba* melody

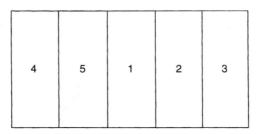

```
                                                    Mi
    Do   Do   Do   Do           Do   Do   Do   Do        Do
Sol                  Sol    Sol
```

or

4	5	1	2	3

Lowest keys on the *Embaire*

Pitch string of the *Okumala Olwemba* melody

```
                                                    3
    1    1    1    1           1    1    1    1        1
4                   4    4
```

FIGURE 2.7   *Ekidha Tobana Kabaliga's* Okumala Olwemba.

In each example the use of "Do" and "1" signifies the principle note of the five-note scale. An alternate means of transcribing this melodic gesture is given immediately below the solfege example. This second solution substitutes numbers for syllables and like the first example, suggests two lower notes in the five-note series added on the lower end of the *embaire*. Below the diagram of the keys is a string of labeled pitches, the melody line in syllables and numbers printed graphically to represent low and high tones. These pitch strings are intended to create a transcription pictograph of that very important musical moment.

ACTIVITY 2.1 *As you listen to the okumala olwemba at the end of CD track 5, follow the transcription in Figure 2.7. You might find it helpful to sing with the recording.*

"Muliranwa" is a sad song typically performed within the context of a larger, evening-long performance. The meaning conveyed in the sung text is intended to be didactic. The song's text focuses on death and suggests several ways to be friendlier with each other since we all travel the same path in life. It advises listeners as to the merits of showing respect for other people, specifically one's neighbors. The *omulesi owolwemba* states that one can have friends in life just as easily as one can have enemies. He continues by suggesting that if someone with whom you are familiar dies, even if they are an enemy, then it is imperative to acknowledge something good and decent about that person.

Later in the performance of "Muliranwa," after a break during which time the dancers join in the music making (Figure 2.8), the *omulesi owolwemba* suggests as he sings that when we ascend to heaven after we die, our friends and family will only have our grave to visit. He advises us that family, friends, and neighbors will soon follow those who die first. Thus he concludes, bridges should not be burned while we are still alive.

On that particular summer evening in rural Busoga in eastern Uganda as I listened to the *omulesi owolwemba* and interwoven texts within the evening-long performance, I noted that many of the improvised lyrics supporting the music and dance reflected current social issues, such as the famine that had recently swept the region and a vote by the national government to mandate universal primary education (U.P.E.) throughout the country. I also began to experience significant

FIGURE 2.8   *Two dancers with traditional cloths wrapped around their waists slowly approach the* embaire *in the Bugwere village ensemble at the* ngoma *session.   (Photo by Gregory Barz.)*

changes in traditional playing styles from what I was accustomed to hearing on historical field recordings—representing for me a critical moment of innovation and adaptation in contemporary *embaire* performance in Busoga.

There are dramatic variations of dynamics, tempo, and intensity throughout the performance of "Muliranwa" heard on this recording, and the shifts between softer and louder sections are just one indication of the importance of timbre as a compositional element in this region of East Africa. Perhaps the most striking innovation in contemporary Busoga *embaire* performance, as mentioned earlier, is the dramatic extension of the wooden slats that are used by a typical ensemble. From an average of 21-keys per instrument, *embaire* have now expanded to include up to 25 keys in several Busoga villages. The new keys—typically added to the lowest register of the instrument—are not played in "traditional" *embaire* fashion, that is with wooden stick mallets. Rather the additional lower keys are pounded upon with clenched fists as one would on drums, adding accents and additional percussive effects to the overall *embaire* ensemble.

Two explanations have been offered to explain this relatively recent innovation to the *embaire* instrument in village ensembles. The first suggests that since making drums is especially time-consuming and expensive, effecting the drum-like extension of the *embaire* is a logical innovation. A second explanation is that *embaire* have always have been an ongoing, developing musical tradition, and the extension of keys should be understood as part of a normative progression.

The first explanation seems to be based largely on economics. As the manufacture of drums becomes increasing expensive and as materials for the drums become scarce in times of famine, the cost of drums precipitates an extension of the *embaire* to include the role of the drum. This explanation is supported by comments made on several occasions. The second explanation centers on change and adaptation as inherent aspects within historical *embaire* tradition. In most cases, the reality is probably somewhere in between the two explanations given. For the Ekidha Tobana Kabaliga Group (as can be seen in Figure 2.9) the extensions of

FIGURE 2.9   *Members of the Ekidha Tobana Kabaliga Group perform on the* embaire. *Mzee Rasidi, leader of the group, is seated at the far right in the white shirt. Six men play the large* embaire, *some with sticks, others on the low end with their fists. The* omulesi owolwemba *(solo singer) stands behind the players.   (Photo by Gregory Barz.)*

the *embaire* keyboard were a personal response by the group's leader, Mzee Rasida, to a lack of drums in the area, a "natural" addition in his words.

Evening *embaire* performances are sites for the negotiation of meaning in Busoga village life; as poor crop conditions and famine spread throughout the area, the communal evening playing of the seven-person *embaire* performances changed functions, embracing a new modality as a tool for social mediation; songs were composed to educate, to advise, and to make meaning out of new, often life-threatening situations. The music of *embaire* becomes the physical embodiment of meaning for many villagers of Busoga.

CASE STUDY #3: KISUMU TOWN, WESTERN KENYA

Excerpt from Fieldnotes. *It was late in the afternoon when I arranged to meet with the singer, Omar Abdallah and his brother Suleiman. Omar seemed reluctant at first to speak English, even though he had completed his secondary education and was fairly fluent. Instead, we conversed in a combination of KiSwahili and Arabic (I later learned that his father is the* munshidin *(chief religious leader) in the local mosque and thus taught his son to recite the Qur'an in Arabic). We discussed the role of music in Islam in Western Kenya, and I specifically asked him about the "nyimbo" (songs) that the Islamic Choir performed at the Muslim Secondary School. He stopped me before I could continue, correcting me. "They were not 'nyimbo' Bwana Gregory. They were 'kaswida' [devotional chants with texts from the Qur'an], and as such, they only enhance the religious sentiment of the text. If they were 'nyimbo,' if they were music, then they would surely distract one from the religious belief."*

Kisumu is a large town along the banks of Lake Victoria in western Kenya. Kisumu is in fact Kenya's second largest town, heavily populated with people of the Luo ethnic group, but many different ethnicities blend in this urban environment. The population is primarily Muslim, but there are also many denominational and breakaway Christian churches in the outlying areas of the town.

During one of my visits with Lawrence Chiteri at the Muslim Secondary School [the man whose definition of ngoma was used to introduce this volume] I could hear the school's Muslim Choir rehearsing across the school compound. When it was time for Chiteri to go teach a class, I took the opportunity to observe the choir. I took a seat as the mixed choir of young men and women finished performing a kaswida. *After greeting several people, I observed the men untying their* habaaya *headscarves, while at the same time the women took off their* hijab *headscarves. The women, however, remained in their traditional, floor-length Muslim* buibui *black robes. As the women gathered in a circle in the center of the room to sing, I immediately recognized the rhythms of the coastal Kenyan* Chakacha *[chakacha literally means, "the rustle of grass when one walks through it"].* Chakacha *is a women's traditional* ngoma. *As a drummer improvised on the set* Chakacha *rhythm each of the women tied cloths around their lower hips and began slowly rotating their hips as they began to dance in a circle.*

Several observers have noted the similarity of *Chakacha* to Middle Eastern "belly dancing" due to the highly rhythmicized rotation of the hips. *Chakacha*, a *ngoma* that originated among the WaSwahili people of coastal Kenya and Tanzania, is accompanied by energetic rhythms that have sensual (perhaps even sexual) overtones for many Kenyans (CD track 6). It is important to note that in addition to its popularity along the coast and islands of Kenya, it has also become a national musical symbol of Kenya and thus it is now taught and performed *throughout* the country, often at weddings. This coastal *ngoma* has also had a significant influence on a particular vocal music style of coastal Kenya known as *taarab*, mentioned in the first chapter, as well as on the *taarab* style of the East African island of Zanzibar (see the map in Figure 1.1); it has been a musical style that has had significant influences on other musical forms and styles.

On CD track 6 you will hear a recording of *Chakacha* performed by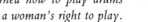
the Muslim Choir from the Muslim Secondary School in Kisumu, a
group from western Kenya in the process of preparing to compete in
secondary school competitions in the capital city, Nairobi, by performing a traditional *ngoma* associated with eastern Kenya. This is a typical
gesture as national identities are constantly affirmed and reaffirmed
through musical performance.

*The young women at the Muslim Secondary School begin
encircling the solo singer as she leads the group in a particular popular song associated with* Chakacha, *accompanied by
a single male drummer. As the singer leaves the group, the
other singers continue dancing in a circle, rotating their hips
as they lift their wrists high above their heads. Another singer
assumes control for the next section of the* ngoma, *and as
she does, the dancers form two lines behind her, dancing back
and forth. A third singer begins and the women reform the
circle. About midway through the Kisumu performance, the
young women again assume the leadership of the drumming
accompaniment from the young man who has taken over.
Rather than neatly concluding the performance of* Chakacha,
the group immediately segues into another version of
Chakacha, *this time performed to a borrowed tune, "Jabala,"
from a neighboring ethnic group in eastern Uganda (you can*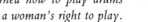
*hear this transition begin at 2:40 on CD track 6). The male
drummer, Omar Abdallah, however, is unfamiliar with the
new song that has been introduced and is unable to fit the*
Chakacha *rhythm into the transitional song. A young
woman, Ziada Mwajuma Bakari, crosses over, pushes Omar
out from behind the drums, and assumes control of the much
more virtuosic drumming demanded of the second half of the
performance. When I raise my eyebrows at Zuleikha
Abubakar, the choir's* mwalimu *[teacher], she laughs and
whispers in my ear that Ziada learned how to play drums
from her mother who felt that it was a woman's right to play.
The lead singer at this point begins calling out in English,
"I love you, I love you" (3:32).*

∞

This performance resonates with the documentation of *Chakacha* along the coast of Kenya by ethnomusicologists Carol Campbell and Carol Eastman:

> Chakacha is also a popular dance done at *harusi*, particularly to celebrate a wedding. It is performed by young women, generally virgins . . . Chakacha is performed in a circle that moves counterclockwise. Each girl folds and ties a *leso* (a piece of brightly colored cloth, also known as *kanga*, usually used as a wrap-around garment) tightly about her hips. The hips are then rotated without any accompanying shoulder movement as the girls progress slowly around the circle. Occasionally, they will stop moving forward but still maintain the hip-rotation. As they dance, they sing the short chakacha songs (Campbell and Eastman 1984, 475).

Musical Transcription. Shown in Figure 2.10 are transcriptions of the *basic* rhythmic pattern that define *Chakacha* presented on CD track 6. The drum plays a continuous pattern that can be understood as consisting of 12 beats, creating a repeating cycle. The transcription of the rhythm typically associated with *Chakacha* that follows is intended only to demonstrate the core pattern. There are other creative variations (and perhaps more interesting) that are presented by the two drummers that are not transcribed in this example.

The transcriptions in Figure 2.10 are based on previous knowledge and experience of the *ngoma* and on observations of Ziada Mwajuma Bakari, the young woman performing at the end of CD track 6. The basic rhythm as performed by the left and right hands of the drummer is offered first (Figure 2.10a). In this example the left hand (L) sounds a low tone on the drum while the right hand (R) sounds a light, higher pitched sound. Another way of "hearing" this rhythm would be as a cycle of 4 beats, with each beat subdivided into three subdivisions; thus, 1-2-3, 2-2-3, 3-2-3, 4-2-3.

In the second transcription (Figure 2.10b), a rhythm that is "pulled" out of this composite rhythm is notated, demonstrating a rhythmic pattern that Ziadi, the drummer, emphasizes both physically and by tone on the drums as she plays. In fact, this composite rhythm or "beats that have been pulled," according to Ziadi, reflect the accents of the dancers at many times during the performance. This more intricate rhythm typically associated with the WaSwahili people can be heard clearly at 0:55. In addition, this rhythm is clearly similar to bell patterns or rhythmic cycles found in other regions of Africa.

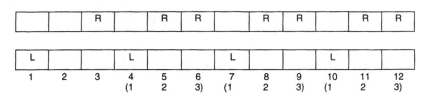

		R		R	R		R	R		R	R
L			L			L			L		
1	2	3	4	5	6	7	8	9	10	11	12
			(1	2	3)	(1	2	3)	(1	2	3)

Note: This particular drummer adopted a personal style of dropping the beat noted above as "2." More often, drummers would play this beat with their right hands.

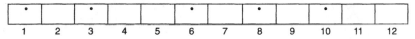

•		•			•		•		•		
1	2	3	4	5	6	7	8	9	10	11	12

FIGURE 2.10 *Transcription of the basic rhythmic pattern that defines this particular ngoma, presented in CD track 6, as* Chakacha. *Note: There are creative variations that are presented by the two drummers in this example. The transcription indicated above is intended only to demonstrate the core pattern.*

The performance of *Chakacha* functions in a very different way in this example, different that is from the dance's original context. In western Kenya the Muslim Choir in Kisumu recontextualizes *Chakacha* as a means of communicating national identity, transferring it from its eastern, coastal context to a western Kenyan context, as a competitive dance to be performed within a national competition circuit for secondary school education.

GENDER AND TRADITIONAL MUSIC PERFORMANCE IN EAST AFRICA

In many regions of East Africa (as in other parts of sub-Saharan Africa and indeed the rest of the world) specific gender roles are prescribed, assumed, or adopted for and by men and women within the contexts of traditional village music making and within musical performance in general. In some areas there are behaviors and beliefs that might appear at first glance to be very different from one's own. Women, for example, are typically discouraged from playing; in some areas of eastern Uganda women are not allowed to play musical instruments. Many men in East Africa believe that women should never play instruments; men typically play instruments and women dance. Some men are of the opinion that women should be discouraged from touching musical instruments, especially drums, or even passing near them. Many young women grow up in villages with the understanding that they are still not supposed to touch any musical instrument and are specifically discouraged from sitting on drums for fear of spoiling the drum by leakage during the period of a women's menstrual cycle. Rather than explaining the reason, men oftentimes merely tell women that they are not allowed near the drums. If they do touch a drum, it is considered a transgression of a social taboo. In fact, even today in many villages in eastern Uganda women are warned not to jump over an instrument such as a drum because it is believed that she will become barren, never being able to produce children.

In urban centers, many of these beliefs are openly challenged, especially in schools where boys and girls are instructed simultaneously on many different musical instruments. Yet, many gender-specific cultural beliefs are deeply rooted. As Centurio Balikoowa, a musician raised in a village culture in eastern Uganda but now living in the urban capital, remarked:

> Women and girls avoiding playing drums has nothing to do with reality. But historically women did not have access to many things, and they used to not put on those undergarments, so if it was time for *that thing* and they sat on a drum, it was believed that it would spoil the what? The drum. But, over time, this translated into a deeply felt belief. Now, for those parents who still have those funny beliefs from the villages, they are not at all happy with their young girls playing the instruments. But, we are trying to educate them that these things represent no problems. But they somehow still aren't convinced. They ask themselves, how can that girl play that instrument? We are trying to get that funny idea out of those people's minds. The youth understand, but those older people, they still maintain those beliefs. While it is allowed in the schools it is still a problem. It is not gone yet.

CONCLUSION

The case studies presented in this chapter from the Busoga region (Uganda), Sukumaland (Tanzania), and Kisumu town (Kenya)—two villages and a town—offer a specific contextualization for the critical issues that are addressed elsewhere in this volume, and consequently provide a focus on the interdependent relationship of drumming, dancing, and singing. In many ways traditional East African performance functions as a social and musical institution, and while not all of the examples offered in this volume fit into the subcategory of traditional music in East Africa, "*ngoma*," it is nevertheless helpful to keep in mind scholar John Janzen's definition of that deeply rooted concept: *Ngoma is* "the term for drum, as well as drumming or other musical instrumentation, singing, dancing, and the complex of constituent behavior and concepts" (Janzen 1992, 290). It is essential to emphasize that whatever local, indigenous term is embraced for traditional musical performance does not signify a music genre or category *per se*, rather what is typically evoked by such terms is a particular environment within which various music genres are generated.

In the chapter that follows, the focus will shift toward other functions and roles of traditional musical performances such as ways in which governments (national and local) often rely on music to communicate social cohesion. Also examined will be ways in which music functions in *both* traditional and innovative ways, such as how performances may often provide a context within which instruction, healing, or religious affirmation occurs. Today traditional musical performances frequently support various forms of entertainment (as will be detailed in subsequent case studies), often separated from their original, historical contexts.

CHAPTER 3

Fostering Social Cohesion: Competition and Traditional Musical Performance

*True communities are built not of dewy affection
or ideological purity but of engagement.*
—Henry Glassie, Passing the Time in Ballymenone *(1982, 282).*

INTRODUCTION: COMPETITION AS SOCIAL COHESION

Traditional musical performances throughout East Africa often occur within highly competitive events, constituting an important form of and contribution to popular entertainment that includes song duels, choir competitions, drumming and dance contests, sporting events, religious rituals, and games. Though competitive music performance is certainly not particular to East Africa, the ability of competitive music making to be a fundamental community-shaping institution in these areas of the African continent is truly significant. The two case studies introduced in this chapter—one rural, one urban—demonstrate the *function* of traditional musical performances in the fostering of *social cohesion*. By addressing social aspects of music making in East Africa, the opportunity is presented to explore how rivalries can serve to solidify friendship while simultaneously expressing senses of community and difference. These case studies demonstrate the significance of music for people in a community as they negotiate the world around them.

A secondary point in this chapter concerns the ability of local, regional, and national forms of traditional music within the context of music competitions to function as the targets for appropriation by larger social forces such as governments or organized institutions of religions. Competitions, for example, are often used to disseminate information related to campaigns by governments and NGOs (Non-Governmental Organizations), and thus have become venues highlighting medical and social issues such as HIV/AIDS, traditional healing, and witchcraft.

Another point to be underscored in this chapter concerns music and power. The period of colonization and indirect rule in East Africa during the nineteenth and twentieth centuries was a time of great distortion of power and immediate shifts in attitudes toward indigenous musical performance were instituted. This distortion of power forced many East Africans to veil identities, systems of belief, and many aspects of expressive culture, including music. While some forms of competitive expressive culture were suppressed, others emerged as creative responses.

The first case study in this chapter will draw from the annual *Bulabo* festival held annually in Sukumaland, Tanzania. *Bulabo* ("little flowers") is a two-week long competition of Sukuma music and dance sponsored by the local Roman Catholic diocese. Officially beginning on the Sunday feast day of Corpus Christi, *Bulabo* typically opens with ceremonious processionals that commence at local churches throughout Sukumaland. (This feast of Corpus Christ is celebrated in the Catholic tradition throughout the world on the Thursday after Trinity Sunday, the first Sunday after Pentecost.) Music and dance competitions that occur as part of the *Bulabo* festival are sites within which community values (not just Catholic social values) are displayed, remembered, and reinforced.

The second case study will extend the discussion to include music that is primarily choral. While the Muslim Choir selection and Basoga "Muliranwa" selections introduced in the previous chapter were also primarily vocal, they nevertheless drew more heavily on indigenous East African vocal performance styles. Contemporary choirs in Tanzania, however, negotiate between multiple cultures and multiple performance traditions—African and European—in their daily performances. Choral music and other communal singing traditions have long been dominant forms of music making in East Africa. Yet, for many people in the past, singing in choirs was clearly interpreted as a veiled *translation* of traditional musics to church settings at times when foreign and local missionary involvement in the area forbade the use of drums and dancing in newly established churches. Contemporary and historical choral music should not, therefore, be understood as lacking traditional music, rather they can be seen as a transformation or extension of the traditional musics in African Christian settings.

CASE STUDY #1: BULABO IN SUKUMALAND, TANZANIA

Excerpt from Fieldnotes. *It is Sunday morning in Nyanhugi.*
The large bell adjacent to the village's Catholic Church rings

out, announcing to the hilltop community and beyond that mass will soon begin. I hear the distant bell from down the mountain in the village of Kisesa where I quickly finish helping a group of men erect a temporary stage in a large, enclosed site that doubles as a soccer stadium. Shortly after hearing the bell I catch a ride to the Bujora Cultural Center in Nyanhugi in the back of a pickup truck along with several other people on their way to the church service. The long path leading up to Nyanhugi is crowded with others headed in the same direction. Women of the Catholic congregation have cleared the path of all debris and plants with their hoes in preparation for the feast day processional that will wind down the mountain. (See Figure 1.1, for a map that includes Tanzania.)

As you listen to CD track 7, a recording of the Bulabo processional down the mountain, follow the listening guide offered in Activity 3.1. This guide breaks down the two-hour-long event into several performance segments.

A large crowd has gathered for a special outdoor mass to celebrate and inaugurate Bulabo, the week-long Sukuma Catholic festival that begins with the observance of the annual Catholic Corpus Christi feast day. Across the church compound a building houses the royal Sukuma thrones, on top of which are kept a collection of royal drums. Elders from neighboring Sukuma communities have gathered on the roof dressed in floor-length white Muslim kanzus to beat the royal drums that will sound the call for the beginning of the Bulabo processional; they await the cue from Father Mugonye. At the end of the three and one-half-hour long mass the elders respond to their cue, and the Holy Eucharist is carried down the mountain in a monstrance, a special ostensorium designed to resemble a traditional Sukuma shield (Figure 3.1). The bearer of the monstrance with the glass-enclosed host wears a leopard skin, a symbol of one of the many royal Sukuma clan's authority.

FIGURE 3.1 *Photograph of the monstrance, a special ostensorium designed to resemble a traditional Sukuma shield.* *(Photo by Gregory Barz.)*

  The procession stops several times as it makes its way down to the Kisesa stadium. At each stop prayers are proclaimed and one of the choirs initiates a song (CD track 7). Each time the processional begins anew a group of young women in red and white matching outfits scatters flower petals along the pathway upon which the church officials, priests, and sisters will follow. The processional down to the stadium (Figures 3.2 and 3.3) and the ceremonial consecration of the soccer stadium as holy signals to the community at large that Bulabo, a week-long series of competitive music and performances has officially begun. Each afternoon during the week that follows, dance groups from throughout Sukumaland compete against each other. While everyday life continues much as it did before, a significant amount of time is set aside each day for socializing and for competitive music and dance performance.

      ∽

ACTIVITY 3.1 *Listening Guide*
Performance segment 1 (0:00–0:45)
  The recording begins at the top of the mountain as the processional commences. Clearly audible in this segment are the royal Sukuma drums played by Sukuma elders on the roof of the building housing the royal Sukuma thrones.
Performance segment 2 (0:46–1:29)
  Several groups of young girls begin to form double lines as the Sukuma elders continue their coordinated drumming. The girls sing a brief chorus as they scatter flower petals (Bulabo) along the pathway. The segment closes with women's ululation, an utterance that expresses the joy and happiness of those involved in the processional.
Performance segment 3 (1:30–2:58)
  The women's ululation continues as several sacristans and altar boys ring bells as they enter the processional. A group of priests and sisters merge into the processional, as do groups of young women with fly whisks made from the tail hair of wildebeest which they wave through the air as they dance. The royal drums cease as a chorus is sung to begin the processional down the mountain.
Performance segment 4 (2:59–3:31)
  The processional begins. Several drummers join the progression of the crowd.
Performance segment 5 (3:32–4:34)
  A drum signal is sounded and the young girls with rose petals stop. They quickly turn around to face the priests and sisters, sing a brief song, and then throw more flower petals along the pathway. The processional quickly become larger and there are now several musical divisions within the greater group. Different segments of the procession have instruments—drums, shakers, and bells. The overlapping occurring within the various groups in the processional's soundscape does not distract the effort.
Performance segment 6 (4:35–6:24)
  The processional has splintered into three distinct groups. At a plateau all groups congregate together and women shout ulula-

tions as they wave to other groups. The groups eventually progress, moving on as they make their way down to the stadium.
Performance segment 7 (6:25–end)
  A group of drummers positions themselves to welcome the processional into the Bulabo stadium. The destination of the processional—a temporary altar constructed at the far end of the soccer stadium—has been reached, and all groups begin encircling the altar as the entire crowd makes its way into the stadium.

The *Bulabo* processional includes segments in which rather appealing parallel singing in intervals of thirds is heard that is a specific harmonization of a melodic, vocal line associated with a European style that follows predictable harmonic patterns. This should be a style of harmonization that many will be familiar with; it has now become a traditional part-singing style in many parts of Africa and can and should be understood as "African."

FIGURE 3.2   *The processional down the mountain.*   *(Photo by Gregory Barz.)*

FIGURE 3.3 *Another angle of the processional down the mountain.* *(Photo by Gregory Barz.)*

While *Bulabo* has existed in various forms throughout Sukumaland since the late 1920s, Father David Clement, the late Canadian missionary priest claimed to have popularized it; ethnomusicologist Frank Gunderson has seen diary entries that confirm that as early as the 1920s the early *Bulabo* festivals were huge events, certainly larger than they are today in Nyanhugi village. In the 1950s, Father Clement advanced experimental projects in which indigenous Sukuma symbols, music, and traditions were purposefully evoked or adapted to the Catholic liturgy. Adaptation was critical in Clement's early teaching mission as well as that of the local Catholic Church that participated heavily in the indigenization or localization of both Sukuma cultural terms and concepts and Catholic materials.

Reconceptualized in 1952 in Nyanhugi village, the site of the present Bujora Cultural Centre, the competitive performances of traditional music that form the core of *Bulabo* were from the very beginning an attempt to both indigenize Catholic spirituality *and* preserve Sukuma traditional culture. *Bulabo* festivals occur today in Catholic parishes throughout Sukumaland, yet the village of Nyanhugi is still looked to by many as an important spiritual home for the transformation of the *Bulabo* performing tradition.

Bulabo takes its name from the Sukuma term for "little flowers" and refers to the flower petals dropped along the pathway leading down to the stadium by young girls during the Holy Day's processional. According to the late Mzee Kang'wina, a Sukuma elder and an original catechist in the early Bujora church who recently passed away, *Bulabo* is an ironic name for the festival, since many if not all of the flowering plants that now grow in the area surrounding Nyanhugi village and that provide the local procession with its petals, were brought to Sukumaland by outside missionaries.

BUFUMU

Before the introduction of Christianity in Sukumaland, there were strong indigenous cultural institutions that offered ritual celebrations that continue today. *Bufumu*, for example, is a generic term used to describe the manipulation of both good and bad divinatory forces in Sukuma culture. *Bufumu* can refer to divination, rainmaking, internal medical healing, witchcraft, and dance medicine, among other things. Several field colleagues—notably those who were Catholic and in positions of authority—attempted to convince the author on several occasions that many culturally significant traditions shifted from local systems of divine power such as *Bufumu* to Christian observations such as *Bulabo* with the introduction of Christianity. Yet, as Frank Gunderson documents, *Bufumu* still exists throughout Sukumaland and is perhaps stronger now than ever (Gunderson 1999). Christianity certainly did not supplant the reliance on or manipulation of divinatory forces despite concerted and organized efforts to do so.

Nevertheless, priests today find *Bulabo* effective for attracting mass audiences (both Catholic and non-Catholic) to celebrate—however on the periphery—Catholic festivals. According to Aimee and Mark Bessire, the intentional mix of Christian religion and traditional Sukuma culture in *Bulabo* has been historically supported by the local and foreign churches as a means by which many Sukuma individuals have been attracted to Catholicism (Bessire and Bessire 1997).

BAGAALU AND THE *BAGIIKA* DANCE SOCIETIES

A typical highlight of the weeklong *Bulabo* festival held in the Kisesa Stadium, as was the case when the festival outlined in this chapter was documented, is the gathering of members of the two traditional Sukuma dance societies for a series of singing competitions. Today, most Sukuma farmer-musicians align themselves with one of two traditional dance societies—the *Bagiika* or the *Bagaalu*—from which they draw their ritual, medicinal, and esoteric musical knowledge (Gunderson 1999 and 2000). These two dance societies have, according to Tanzanian historian Elias Songoyi, a "joking relationship and the tradition is based on what the Sukuma call *wilingi*, a kind of singing that seeks to scandalize the opponent" (Songoyi 1990, 31).

The tradition of competitive singing, called *wigaashe*—typically translated as "sitting song"—involves members of each dance society led by the individual society's composer. The tradition exists in contexts other than *Bulabo*. The composers of the two societies simultaneously lead their groups in pre-composed materials that praise the achievements of individual members of the society. At the first *Bulabo* festival the author attended in 1999 there were several improvisatory moments based on a tradition of trading insults during the *wigaashe*, and in this case specifically regarding the author's presence at the event. But *wigaashe* compositions have traditionally highlighted fixed and highly rehearsed feats of memory. This tradition of trading insults goes back to the time, for example, when *wigaashe* composers were judged on their ability to recite the same *wigaashe* poem-song twice in a row, precisely without deviation.

SAMBA

Excerpt from Fieldnotes. *On the day of the initial wigaashe competition in 1999 I arrive at the Kisesa stadium early and find members of the Bagiika dance society busily marking off their group's territory with samba, strong charms meant to protect the performers and attract the appreciation of the crowd. I approach a young man burning a collection of herbs in a hollowed cow's horn in the center of the group's designated performance area. He explains to me that the herbs are a strong* samba *or medicine that would protect the members of the Bagiika society from any similar samba brought to the competition by the rival Bagaalu. Members of both societies eventually paraded into the Kisesa stadium as the sun begins to set, and each group sits on benches constructed of felled trees. The two societies sit adjacent to each*

other and begin an evening of competitive wigaashe. *On other festival days, groups gather from throughout Sukuma-land to compete against each other. Success does not result from strict adjudication, rather it is typically determined by the ability of a group to attract a crowd to its performance area and thus attain the crowd's approval. In its Bujora in-carnation,* Bulabo *relies less on this, and it is well known for its innovation in this regard, as no winners are officially declared. There are no adjudicators present, and cash awards are typically split equally among all participants. Those groups who fail to attract audiences often make accusations of* samba, *or magical applications.*

Mbiina groups from the *Bagaalu* and the *Bagiika* dance societies com-peting against each other often use three types of *sumbu.*

- Magic to attract audiences
- Magic to protect against the application of magic from rival groups
- Blatant or overt witchcraft used against the opponent

Upon listening to CD track 8 you will hear members of both the *Bagiika* and *Bagaalu* societies competing as they perform simultaneously. The composers of each group, dressed in elaborate and complementary costumes, lead the simultaneous singing of the two groups. Members of the groups clap rhythms and women ululate to express their joy. There is constant conversation in the background as members of each society discuss the day's events on the sidelines. The sounds projected from a nearby showing of a kickboxing movie can be heard in the back-ground along with the sound of dice rolling at nearby gambling tables. In this audio example performance spaces often blur as one group at-tracts an audience by disrupting the progress of another group (for a representation of these malleable performance venues see Figure 3.4).

CHANGES AND ADAPTATION IN *BULABO*

As this first case study suggests, significant changes have occurred in the fifty-year history of *Bulabo* performances at Bujora. Of these, per-haps the most notable has been professionalization. What was once an open and casual series of competitions with food and sustenance the

FIGURE 3.4 *Photograph of dueling dance ensembles as they compete for audience attention and participation.* *(Photo by Gregory Barz.)*

primary source of remuneration in exchange for participation, has become a significant financial burden for local churches. Simultaneously, *Bulabo* has become a moneymaking opportunity for competitors from local areas and beyond. In addition, *mbiina* groups increasingly expect to be remunerated for the high costs of transport and sustenance. These changes also affect the typical length of the annual *Bulabo* festival; what was formerly an extended competition held for several weeks is often reduced to a week-long event (or shorter) due to the lack of funds to support the historically larger effort.

Much of the 1999 *Bulabo* festival season was devoted to a week-long series of meetings between elders from various Sukuma communities and elders of Maasai communities from territories bordering on Sukumaland with the intended goal of establishing a dialogue. With funding provided by a Danish nongovernmental organization, the two groups of elders met daily with the specific goal of finding some way to approach an amelioration of conflict between Maasai and Sukuma over recent and ongoing cattle thefts between the two ethnic groups. At the end of each day's meetings, the two groups of elders would travel together down from the Bujora Center to the Kisesa Stadium to witness and participate in the *Bulabo* festivities. One of the younger Maasai leaders, Lazaro Ole Kosyando, indicated on several occasions that *Bulabo*, and specifically the competitive *mbiina* segments of the festival, might be the only way the two groups could reconcile and come together. On the final day of the 1999 *Bulabo* celebration, Joseph Lupande, representing the Sukuma delegation, announced to the gathered crowd in the Kisesa Stadium that the *Bulabo 2000* festival would be devoted to welcoming Maasai dancers to the festival held at Kisesa Stadium. *Bulabo* in this regard continues to function as a forum for adaptation; adaptation that at one time was an attempt at maintaining Sukuma culture from within, is now more concerned with reaching out.

In the introduction to *Enchanting Powers* (Sullivan 1997), Lawrence Sullivan suggests that religious music is particularly capable of empowerment, especially in its ability, its mimetic capacity, to accommodate other realities within its performance as well as stimulate and inspire other realities. It is within the performance of rituals that the political and the sacred often combine in their effort to create a symbiotic blend that becomes a unifying tradition, or put more simply, a musical fusion, as Philip Bohlman suggests elsewhere in *Enchanting Powers*.

Throughout *Dancing Prophets*, Steven Friedson's ethnography of music and healing among the Tumbuka people of Malawi in Southern Africa, specific traditional music-dances are analyzed that function in similar ways to the *mbiina* described above from Tanzania. The performance of music and religion among the Tumbuka often occurs within a coextensive moment in which spirit possession is enacted in order to achieve healing. According to Friedson, "For the Tumbuka speaking peoples of northern Malawi , musical experience is the structural nexus where healer, patient and spirit meet" (Friedson 1996, xvi). Dancing prophets, singing patients, and drummed spirits—together, music, medicine, and spirituality contribute to the healing process of the people's lives among the Tumbuka.

One of the primary purposes of *Bulabo* is the creation of sacred ritual spaces within which elements of *both* traditional and Christian Sukuma culture are performed, re-created, adapted, and most importantly, empowered. Yet, in many ways the sacred power of *Bulabo*, if viewed as a form of religious music, often draws its strength from the very promotion of Sukuma culture that Sullivan might understand as facilitating and incorporating external realities. Such contemporary realities, whether understood as external or internal, are critical to the celebration of *Bulabo* at the Bujora Centre, and are provoked into resonance, especially in *wigaashe* song competitions between the Bagiika and Bagaalu dance societies, and in *mbiina* dance and music competitions. What was at one time a celebration of the Catholic feast of Corpus

Christi, *Bulabo* today has been extended to offer significant opportunities for intracultural mediation. The indigenization of sacred power is far-reaching within the festival that now provides a forum for approaching conflict and difference between inter-African rather than intra-Sukuma cultures.

In this case study it is suggested that *Bulabo* incorporates Sukuma *mbiina*, and thus draws on the power (and authority) of traditional performance practices. *Bulabo* also demonstrates that cultural processes we label as indigenization or adaptation often neither follow only one direction nor do they involve a shift of sacred power in specific cultural performances. There certainly were systems within which sacred power was evoked in Sukumaland, for example, long before the arrival of European and North American missionaries.

CASE STUDY #2: CHOIR COMPETITIONS IN DAR ES SALAAM

Choir competitions in Dar es Salaam, Tanzania's largest city, located on the Indian Ocean, are typically all-day, highly structured, much anticipated performance events that take place on designated Sundays at centrally located churches. Choir competitions offer a window through which we can focus on the social cohesion of choir communities that occurs within musical performance, communities that are seldom included in a representation of history or music in Africa. (Notable exceptions have been the contributions of John Blacking: 1980, 1987.)

A choir competition is a rigorous gathering with participation typically determined by elaborate ranking systems based on outcomes of previous competition seasons. The two principal goals of a competition—to compete (and of course to win) and to sing the praises of God—do not represent a conflict in the minds of the competitors. They are, in fact, interdependent, since competitions provide opportunities for fellowship between choirs, exposure to new and varied musical repertoires, guidance and encouragement from more experienced judges and teachers, spiritual fulfillment, and *fun*!

Competitions consist of rounds of poetic recitations, dramatic presentations, and Bible readings, yet the main focus is usually on the final choir performance. The choir events usually begin on early Sunday afternoons and often continue (depending on the number of choirs scheduled to compete) into the early evening. From ten to twenty choirs compete in these festivals, with each choir performing a set song and two optional songs. Choirs rehearse for months in advance of a competition, spending considerable time learning new songs, coaching new choir members on ways to win and "brushing off" old songs, a phrase used to refer to the process of relearning songs that have not been in a choir's repertoire for quite some time.

So, why include a case study on *choral* music performances in a volume about traditional musical performances? The answer is complicated, the clearest single response would underscore the subjugation of many traditional musical forms in East Africa by both missionaries and colonial officials. New vocal genres were introduced in churches over time, and today these vocal genres have embraced traditional musics in an emergent art form often thought to have all but replaced such traditions in many communities.

Three stories are now offered that illustrate ways in which Tanzanian choirs continue to assert their main function—to provide a cohesive community—within competitions that represent the choirs' ongoing negotiation with colonial and missionary histories over the past century. The music examples included in these vignettes also tell a story of three critical moments in the development and syncretic reinterpretation of Tanzanian choirs, each with a distinct association with traditional musical performances in the area.

• *Vignette 1.* In the first vignette, specific aspects of contemporary Tanzanian choir performance are identified that deliberately reference the initial evangelical encounter in the late nineteenth-century. This case study demonstrates the music that was used by European cultures in many cases to replace indigenous musical performances.

• *Vignette 2.* The second vignette presents the emergence of Tanzanian voices in the period between the two World Wars—from the end of WWI (1918) until the beginning of WWII (1939).

• *Vignette 3.* The third vignette focuses on changes in choir music since the postcolonial era in the 1960s, the indigenization of choral music in East Africa, and the introduction of drums and other musical instruments into church contexts.

VIGNETTE 1: THE INITIAL EVANGELICAL ENCOUNTER

Excerpt from Fieldnotes. *I board a* daladala *(small inner-city bus) headed for downtown from my flat in Mlimani. The*

side doors are open, and since there are no seats available, I hang on the outside of the vehicle, talking with the bus conductor for most of the ride. Once downtown, I make my way on foot through the dusty side streets of the Kariakoo district of Dar es Salaam. It is the least safe area of town, and I nervously clutch my bag of recording equipment as I head toward the choir competition at the district's Lutheran church. Several vehicles crammed full of choir members drive past me, negotiating the enormous potholes of the streets. "Habari? Karibu!" ["How are you? Welcome!"], they shout in my direction as I wave in return.

Outside the church compound a choir climbs off their dal-adala, singing and clapping. There are several other vehicles parked outside the compound. I stop to greet familiar choir leaders as I pass through the outer crowd into the church. The smells from the nearby kiosks where vendors fry chips tempt me as I contemplate whether I have time to grab some food. It is noon and the sun is fierce. One of my field colleagues from the choir at the Buguruni Lutheran Church runs up to me, joking that only wazungu, only white people stand out in the sun and heat like this. He grabs my hand and we walk into the church hand in hand.

Inside the church, the loud, wheezing of the low-hanging ceiling fans offers little relief to the crowd gathered for the all-day competition. Sounds of excitement come from the choirs as they visit with each other, fix each other's robes, test and tune drums over small flames, and fill out last-minute adjudication sheets for the judges. A choir member rushes up and offers me a plate of fresh mangoes and mandarin oranges, and I am overcome with the smell of fresh fruit. I decline at first. The smell of the mandarins wins, however, and I walk down the main aisle with the plate of fruit in hand.

There are several people in charge of the competition, and each comes to welcome me. "Karibu Profesa Barz, karibu ndani" ["Welcome Professor Barz, welcome inside"]. Soon the master of ceremonies checks the sound system and asks the choirs to take their assigned positions within the pews. Hosea Mwambapa, himself a victorious choir director from a previous round of competitions, is asked to warm up the com-

peting choirs by rehearsing the "set song," a required piece to be performed by all choirs in the competition. Mwambapa rushes up to the master of ceremonies, shaking his hand as he thanks him for the honor. His shoes are newly painted with white kiwi shoe polish and he wears a matching white patent leather belt. He appears nervous about the heavy responsibility of leading the congregated choirs as he wipes the perspiration off his face, then reaches into his pocket for a pitch pipe to give the assembled choirs their starting pitches.

The sounds of the hymn, "Mahali ni Pazuri" ("This Place is Beautiful" or "Wie Lieblich ist's hienieden" in the original German), immediately fill the church, by then packed to near capacity with sixteen choirs and their supporters. All choirs sing the original four-part harmony of the early nineteenth-century German hymn, and the open-air brick walls of the church seem to expand with the sounds of the choirs out into the neighborhood streets (CD track 9).

As the hymn continues, Aminieli Mkichwe sits next to me in the front pew; we hold hands as we exchange greetings. Mkichwe, teacher of the youth choir at Ubungo Lutheran Church is perhaps the most recognized authority on Lutheran choir music in the Dar es Salaam area. I ask him about the hymn, "Mahali ni Pazuri," specifically why a nineteenth-century German hymn would be chosen as the set song for such an important competition. He tells me that a German hymn or chorale is usually selected as the set piece, and that the choirs are committed to use the competition as an opportunity to learn the old German hymns that have "fallen out of memory."

VIGNETTE 2: THE EMERGENCE OF TANZANIAN VOICES

Excerpt from Fieldnotes. *The choir from Mikocheni Anglican Church, the first to compete in the Anglican competition, stands in their pews on a cue from their director. After singing one verse of their entrance piece the choir turns sharply*

*toward the center aisle and begins a slow, jaunty, and highly
stylized jive processional. The choir smiles and engages the
audience, comprised mostly of other choirs, as they progress
down the aisle toward the altar that serves as the main stage.
Several choir members carry drums, cowbells, and several large
pieces of wood with soda bottle caps nailed to them [used as
a rattle].*

*As the choir reaches the stage the teacher takes his time
arranging the choir, making sure that he achieves the proper
spacing. After performing the required set song, several women
leave their places and arrange themselves on the ground in
front of the choir around a large wooden mortar. Two men
from the back row of the choir come out and hand the women
large wooden pestles. The director begins the choir's first optional African songs by conducting the two women pounding
the pestles into the large mortar in a rhythmic pattern, back
and forth. One of the other judges smiles as he turns to me
saying, "Ah, this conductor here, he is Mhehe from Iringa."
"This is African music," he tells me. The sounds of the percussive mortar and pestle carry throughout the church. The
crowd responds by cheering their affirmation and approval
(CD track 10).*

VIGNETTE 3: A POSTCOLONIAL MOMENT

Excerpt from Fieldnotes. *I arrive at the Kantate choir competition at the Msasani Lutheran Church early and share a
meal of cooked chicken and rice with the Msasani host choir.
At one point two directors, Joachim Kisasa and Erneza
Madeghe, join me. After we finish our meal a young woman
from the choir approaches us with a pitcher of water and a
bowl for washing our hands. As we walk up the hill to the
church together, I ask them if there will be a difference with
this competition since no scoring or ranking of choirs is
planned. Kisasa confirms that there will, in fact, be a significant difference, and namely that the choirs will take greater*

risks by performing music that is more "African." Choirs will mostly perform original Tanzanian compositions, not adaptations of European hymns or songs.

Later, when the time comes for the Kariakoo youth choir to compete, they take a considerable amount of time setting up. I observe several choir members attaching pickup microphones to two large malimba *[plucked lamellophones]. When the time comes for the choir's optional "African" piece, several men move to join two kneeling* malimba *players, forming a small percussion ensemble. The choir performs a song imitating the highly distinctive musical style of the Wagogo ethnic group of central Tanzania (CD track 11).*

A malimba *player sits on the floor in front of the choir directly below the teacher. He plays one amplified* malimba *with a differently tuned* malimba *on the floor for the song's second section. A drummer is seated in the center with a* kayamba *rattle player to right. The women of the choir hold matching rice winnowers that they later place on the ground in order to dance.*

Carol Muller's ethnography of Nazarite women's performance in South Africa (Muller 1999), introduces several ways in which we can understand and appreciate similar phenomenon in another region of sub-Saharan Africa. Specifically, Muller documents this by outlining three ways in which choral performance can be viewed as a coextensive moment of music and religion. The first "moment" involves the historical manipulation of the mission Bible by the group's founder, Isaiah Shembe, to "authenticate his creation of ritual and liturgy." The second moment revolves around the rituals of purity involving sacred songs concerned with the sacrifice of sexual desire. The third moment involves the contemporary commodification of Nazarite spirituality, offering another significant model for understanding the indigenization of music and religion in African contexts.

In the three brief vignettes presented, the musical interaction of contemporary Tanzanian choir members with specific historical moments of musical interaction between European and African sensibilities is illustrated on a fundamental level: first—the nineteenth-century penetration of "German East Africa" by external, European forces; second—the withdrawal of German missionaries from Tanganyika during World

War II; and third—the period of post-Independence for the Republic of Tanzania in the 1960s. Tanzanian choirs actively participated in and directly contributed to the development of unique styles of liturgical performance as early as the last two decades of the nineteenth century. Contemporary choirs interact with the past as they perform new forms of music and new identities that negotiate between multiple cultures and multiple ideologies.

CONCLUSION

This chapter introduces several basic ways that outline how competitions in contemporary East Africa draw upon historical memory while at the same time projecting new, indigenized social identities. Thus new layers of social cohesion are presented for choirs as indigenous communities in East Africa. Competitions function as important sites for the negotiation of historical continuity and modernity within a choir community, and thus can and should be understood as creative African responses.

The history of competitive musical performances is only one thread in the complex tapestry of East African cultural history. This thread, however, is brightly colored and often easy to identify in the weave of contemporary East African life. To understand fully the issues raised in this chapter, other studies of competitive musical performance are needed, such as rural-based seasonal dance competitions, Muslim singing competitions, and the content of school speech and drama competitions among others. Gathering such a plurality of musical case studies would broaden our knowledge of the processes of diffusion and adaptation that have occurred in Kenya, Tanzania, and Uganda over the past one hundred years, thus expanding our general appreciation for both the generalities and particularities of contemporary East African expressive culture.

CHAPTER 4

Individuals in East African Musical Worlds: Gideon Mdegella and Centurio Balikoowa

*I am a simple man. I make music because I must
I sing because I must. I compose because I must.*

Gideon Mdegella

*I don't know where this talent came from. I play because I must play. I
cannot stop. I must sing, and there will always be more songs to sing.*

Centurio Balikoowa

INTRODUCTION

The two case studies detailed in this chapter present very different issues related to the lives and musical careers of two East African musicians—Gideon Mdegella of Tanzania and Centurio Balikoowa of Uganda. As the chapter title suggests, both of these musicians live today in multiple musical worlds, fulfilling numerous musical roles and expecting of themselves to be able to communicate in multiple musical languages. Both musicians have responded well to the needs and demands of modern, urban, and rural contexts in this part of the world. As Mdegella says, he works hard to create music that communicates something of his community's social experience, the way that people "normally feel when they do things in their own way, making them feel more at home." Balikoowa works within a national educational system that encourages (in fact demands) that he be multimusical, that is, fluent in multiple musical languages, and that he teach multimusicality.

Musicians in East Africa today must respond creatively to many demands, including the growing urbanization of the areas in this region, the hierarchies of educational and religious institutions, the rise of the popular music industry, the growth of (and changes) in the recording industry, and the increase of cross-ethnic group interactions. The two case studies offered in this chapter detail the contributions of Mdegella and Balikoowa to these demands, demonstrating two very important responses.

Traditional village music is now encouraged in competitions and music festivals (as detailed in the previous chapter) that take place in elementary and primary schools held throughout the country in rural and urban contexts. Today the best traditional performers (musicians and dancers) in many parts of East Africa are thought to emerge from within this system of competitions. Children are encouraged to learn multiple traditional music styles and instruments from different ethnic groups and areas of their country in order to meet the requirements of local, regional, and national adjudication. Large ensembles of musical instruments are now found in many schools, representing an invented tradition that in many cases would not be found in village performance contexts. These ensembles are often formed in order to meet the requirements of representing as many musical traditions of a given country as possible.

In East African villages the division between audience and performer within the performances of traditional music is not as strict as in contemporary urban contexts. If the playing of the *embaire* (xylophone) in Uganda, for example, is thought to be not quite right in a village you might find someone picking up a stick and joining in, in order to make things sound right and add a musical opinion. Everyone participates in village music making either by clapping, ululating, or by dancing. In villages, a distance is not created between an audience and performers. Only in urban contexts is there more of a distinction, particularly in the performance of traditional musics.

The transmission of traditional musical cultures in East Africa has been a serious issue for musicians such as Gideon Mdegella and Centurio Balikoowa, both of whom communicate here that not enough effort has been made by East Africans themselves to record, document, and preserve the historical value of village traditions. Music and dance are not typically written down or notated in villages; they are preserved in oral traditions. *"Our books are the old people,"* according to Balikoowa:

> We don't have music books where everything is written down, where you could pick it up and play on your own. So, our books are the old people. This is where we get our knowledge. This is where we get

knowledge of our culture and our traditions. From the elders. When they die, then that will be the end. So, we don't have recordings that go back to the beginning. We don't have recordings that document the development of our traditions or how our traditional musical performances have changed over time.

In Uganda some musicians attempt to record locally, but what they typically document are popular or so-called syncretic music traditions (such as the popular Tatunane band in Tanzania and Percussion Discussion and the Big Five bands in Uganda). What has not been preserved, according to Balikoowa, is the fast disappearing traditional music making of villages throughout East Africa. The roots of *original* traditional musics—if such an idea can indeed be said to exist—of many villages are very deep. Many of the villages in which the author has worked are, for example, far from where the tarmac stops, far from where the electricity lines end, and this is where Balikoowa says lies the "real, *original* music" of East Africa.

Traditional music making in general serves important ritual and routine purposes throughout East Africa. For example, musical performances are organized, maintained, planned, and used for the following purposes in the village of Kibaale-Busiki, Uganda:

• *Funeral Rites.* Musical ceremonies facilitate a community's bidding farewell to a community member.

• *Communication.* Specific drumming patterns can be sounded to communicate messages, such as announcing a death in the village. Such drumming participates in the transmission of an immediately understood metalinguistic mode of communication.

• *Labor.* Music making often aids with communal work—such as when drumming, dancing, or singing—providing a steady rhythm.

• *Timekeeping.* Drums are sounded to announce special occasions and times for church services. There is often a drum played on Sunday mornings to alert villagers that a service will soon begin. The drum is played again shortly thereafter to announce the beginning of the service. ("You know, Gregory, not everyone can afford to wear a watch in my village," states Balikoowa).

• *Therapeutic Response.* Music is also used in the Kibaale-Busiki village to address personal problems. The local *endere* (flute), for example, might be played for someone who has been sad for a significant amount of time. The music is thought to create a therapeutic effect on the listener.

- *Didactic Response.* Music can be used to tell stories and educate. If it becomes known that a villager is a known thief or has committed some other crime such as murder, for example, music is used to alert the community and to encourage the individual to change their ways. Rather than addressing social issues directly, music is used to affect change indirectly. Music is a polite, socially acceptable mode for handling social problems in the village.

- *Educational Purposes.* Music, dance, and drama are important tools for coping with HIV/AIDS in Kibaale-Busiki. Instead of telling someone directly how they should or should not behave sexually, acting and singing are engaged to communicate specific stories about people dying. After dramatizing the physical process of death, people are encouraged to go home and reconsider issues concerning AIDS. According to Balikoowa, "most people in Kibaale-Busiki don't listen to everyday speech, but everyone will listen to music and learn. People get the message through music!"

- *Entertainment.* Music accompanies relaxation or contributes to the soundscape of a social atmosphere.

VIGNETTE 1: GIDEON MDEGELLA

Excerpt from Fieldnotes. *As I make my way on foot down Maktaba Street from the post office toward the waterfront in Dar es Salaam, Tanzania, I am nearly hit by what I assume to be a crazed bicyclist. I fall against a parked car, and as I collect myself I realize that whoever pushed me had also called out my name. I quickly realize that it must have been Gideon Mdegella on his old black Chinese bicycle riding off down the street. I spot him in the distance as he waves back at me, and I can tell, even at this distance, that his shoulders are shaking with laughter. When I arrive at the Azania Front Cathedral, I look across the rows of the members of* Kwaya ya Upendo *("The Love Choir") at Mdegella sitting off to the side with a sly smile on his face. I greet him with respect and he welcomes me in response, not breaking his concentration. He continues to hum as he plays a drum with his left hand while writing the rhythm intensely in his songbook with his right hand.*

VIGNETTE 2: CENTURIO BALIKOOWA

Excerpt from Fieldnotes. *I attempt to keep up with Centurio Balikoowa as he runs between several of the classrooms at the Police Children's School in Kampala, clutching the notebook that never leaves his side. Children practice a dance routine in one classroom, while a group of harp players rehearse in another. All around are the sounds of Ugandan traditional music making, with one man, Balikoowa, in charge of it all. "Don't worry Professor," Balikoowa addresses me, "you too will play your* endingidi *(tubefiddle) this well very shortly," as we pass by a room full of eager* endingidi *players. Our conversation is interrupted as he grabs the sticks out of the hands of a young xylophone player and demonstrates the proper way to "mix" a secondary melody.*

COMMUNITIES AND MUSICAL SPECIALISTS

In textbooks and ethnographies about African music, individual musicians are often masked behind labels that characterize anonymous individual behavior as collective behavior. Musicians and dancers are represented as generalized groups, such as when "*The* Wagogo" or "*The* Baganda" or "*The* Luo" feel, react, tell stories, or perform. Many books (even to this day!) include photographs of musicians with labels such as, "African man playing a flute." To address this concern, we must approach a consideration of the role(s) of the individual musical or ritual specialist *within* a specific culture or community. One goal of such an effort should be understanding the many ways musical cultures in East Africa have of distinguishing sharply, gradually, or not at all between the great and the ordinary.

Many communities in East Africa collectively choose to empower a single individual (or group of individuals) to act as ritual or musical specialists. Once chosen, this individual often develops (or is encouraged to develop) particular skills and is empowered by a community to assume authority to lead its important rituals or musical celebrations. Gideon Mdegella and Centurio Balikoowa are just two of a myriad of such individuals working within communities throughout East Africa. It should be noted, however, that the case studies introduced in this chapter may very well not apply to other African contexts; the goal here

FIGURE 4.1　*Photograph of Gideon Mdegella.　(Photo by Gregory Barz.)*

is to dig deeper into the role(s) of particular musical individuals, assigned to them by their communities and their cultural peers.

GIDEON MDEGELLA: "*MWALIMU*"

One day Gideon Mdegella (Figure 4.1), my mwalimu
*["teacher"] and I made our way along the dusty back roads
of the Upanga district in Dar es Salaam, Tanzania, on our
way to a recording session at the Don Bosco recording stu-
dio. As we walked, I attempted to bring our conversation
around to specific aspects of his musical compositions. My
questions were not immediately understandable to Mdegella,
and his responses were not immediately clear to me. I was
asking Mdegella, a specialist in the music and liturgy of a*

particular African church-based choir tradition, to reflect on his skills and talents by using my social constructs, my vocabulary, and my ways of understanding musical sound. It took quite a bit of time—over a year—for Mdegella and me to "understand" each other as well as to feel comfortable enough with each other to develop a mutual way of talking about "music."

Gideon Mdegella's name is synonymous with choir music in Dar es Salaam. He is considered by many to be an advisor, a leader, a composer, an organizer of choir competitions, and a representative of choirs to the local Lutheran Diocese. In addition, he serves as musical director and conductor of *Kwaya ya Upendo,* one of Tanzania's most highly recognized Lutheran choirs. Mdegella composes *nyimbo* ("songs") that are extremely popular, and his *nyimbo* typically cross denominational boundaries, sung by non-Lutheran choirs throughout Dar es Salaam and in other parts of Tanzania. His honesty and fairness complement his musical talent, knowledge, and expertise, and he possesses, in the eyes of many, the essential qualities of a *mwalimu wa kwaya* [teacher, leader, conductor of a choir].

Mwalimu wa Kwaya: *Ritual-Musical Specialists in the Tanzanian Lutheran Church.* While pastors or evangelists in the Tanzanian Lutheran Church handle most liturgical matters, musical elements of liturgy are usually the responsibility of the *mwalimu wa kwaya* ("teacher" or "conductor" of a choir). The roles of the *mwalimu* within the hierarchical structure of the choir and within the organization of the church vary with each community, yet it is usually a well-defined position. A *mwalimu wa kwaya* must constantly negotiate between artistic responsibilities and involvement in the leadership or "social control" of a choir. In addition to assuming the roles of *mbunifu* ["designer of music"] and *msanifu* ["composer"] of music, the *mwalimu* also participates in the leadership of the choir. The principal difference between *mbunifu* and *msanifu* is that the *mbunifu* typically "arranges" music that has been composed by another *msanifu.* The two terms are often conflated, however, and used by many people to refer to the same person.

Mwalimu wa kwaya	"teacher" or "conductor" of a choir
Walimu [wa kwaya]	plural of "*mwalimu*"
Mbunifu	"designer of music," an arranger of music
Msanifu	"composer" of music

Gideon Mdegella is not a "professional" *mwalimu*, at least not professional in what might be our sense of the term. No *mwalimu* is able to support himself or herself financially by working with choirs. No *mwalimu* known to the author receives remuneration for their efforts, time, and participation in a choir. Rather, being a *mwalimu wa kwaya* is conceptualized as a part of normal, everyday life. There is a common assumption among choirs that if one has the talent to compose, arrange, or "design" songs, then these talents will be passed along to a choir community. Talent is fostered, and anyone showing an interest in learning the tools of the trade is usually taken under another *mwalimu's* wing and trained.

"I Am Able to See Very Far, but I Am Unable to Reach There."
Mdegella's broad, expressive face is often smiling either in reaction to a joke or pun he has just offered. He is a distinguished member of the WaHehe ethnic group from the Iringa mountain region of central Tanzania. "Ours is a village of singers. You could compare it to South Africa," according to Mdegella. As a member of *Kwaya ya Upendo* once commented, Mdegella's family name communicates to all Tanzanians that he is of the royal WaHehe family. He settled in Dar es Salaam after a series of failed attempts to further his secondary education in Iringa town. He is a certified accountant, husband and father of five children, and he acts as the chief representative for his extended family within the Dar es Salaam region. Mdegella has participated in the historical and contemporary development of music in the Tanzanian Lutheran Church in both rural and urban environments. He was active in rural church choirs during the end of the era when his country was a British protectorate, and through the period of transition to independence in 1964. He continues his work with urban church choirs now. (Note: Tanganyika became independent in 1961; Zanzibar in 1963. The two nations merged in 1964 as the United Republic of Tanganyika and Zanzibar and changed names to Tanzania later in the year.)

Gideon Mdegella, born in 1946, grew up in a small village outside Iringa town at the foot of the Mzungwa mountain range in Central Tanzania (then "Tanganyika," while under British protection). He is the seventh of fourteen children. His first, native language was KiHehe, the language of the WaHehe people, and he remembers as a young boy singing German hymns in church in the KiHehe language. He learned KiSwahili—which would become the national language of independent Tanzania—only later, while in school. Mdegella has participated in a long history of negotiations between linguistic and musical traditions in his country. He composes songs in multiple musical languages, as he comfortably moves between compositional styles from Southern Africa, Europe, North America, West Africa, and East Africa. Embracing a multinational approach to choir musical composition is not a problem for Mdegella or for most Tanzanian *walimu* (singular, "*mwalimu*") of his generation. Yet, this does not prevent an "Mdegella" style to emerge in his musical compositions rooted in his own musical culture, in the musical style of the WaHehe people of Tanzania. It should be noted, however, that *walimu* of the younger generation, frequently reject the inherited musical styles from Europe, embracing solely musical traditions rooted in African cultures.

Mdegella learned early in his life that he could depend only on himself for his education. When he became interested in music he sought help, but he mostly educated himself, teaching himself to read Western staff notation, sight sing, play keyboard instruments, and compose *nyimbo za kwaya* ("choir songs") in many styles. He is proficient in oral/aural realms of African musical discourse as well as Western musical transcriptional and notational styles.

The title Mdegella embraces with the most pride is that of *mwalimu*, given to him by *Kwaya ya Upendo*. It is a title that directly translated means, "teacher," yet implies much more. The responsibilities of a *mwalimu wa kwaya* do not correspond directly to those of an American "choir director." A Tanzanian *mwalimu* is expected to be responsible for the following:

- compose songs for the choir
- teach the songs to the choir
- conduct the choir during Sunday services and other events
- preserve the repertoire of the choir in his or her memory

As *mwalimu* for *Kwaya ya Upendo*, Mdegella is expected to compose, create, arrange, and teach new musical materials almost every day of each week. The reason for the constant demand for new material, as Mdegella suggests below, is that choirs such as *Kwaya ya Upendo* become easily "bored" or under-stimulated without a constant, ongoing flow of new material.

In the following sections, transcriptions of excerpts from field interviews are presented that are intended to provide a sense of Mdegella's perspective of himself. Field interviews are quoted extensively. The transcriptions are intended to allow the original conversations to be "read" with some inflections of the original spoken event, following a set of conventions for ethnopoetic transcriptions adapted from ethnomusicologist Jeff Titon (Titon 1988, 316) and others, detailed below.

Roman typeface—ordinary conversational volume

Italic typeface—decreased level of volume

New line—breath or pause

[   ] Brackets—indicate nonverbal communication

< >—a visual symbol for laughter, or a smile in the voice

AUTHOR: Gregory Barz

    GM: Gideon Mdegella

AUTHOR: So, what makes you
        continually compose new pieces
        of music
        even if the choir can't do them justice?
        what keeps you going?

    GM: I have to keep on singing

AUTHOR : You have to keep on singing
        what happens if you stop singing?
        what happens if you stop composing?

    GM: Why?

AUTHOR: What will happen if you stop composing?
        or, if you stop singing?

    GM: The singing would be boring
        yeah
        the singing would be
        they'd get bored
        by singing the same pieces all along
        so, the whole thing would be boring and < > I would
          definitely disappoint them
        coming for the rehearsals means having something new
        I think that is
        normal human nature
        we always go for new things
        almost in everything
        you're used to putting yourself in a style of shirt
        you'd like to have something new
        yeah

The majority of materials introduced to *Kwaya ya Upendo* by Mdegella are original compositions. The constant demand by the choir for this type of creativity is critical in understanding the role of the *mwalimu*. This is perhaps a result of the aesthetic of music in oral traditions; a song is "old" immediately after it is sung. There is a much greater and more immediate emphasis placed on *new* musical compositions.

In addition to his strengths as a leader and organizer within his community, Gideon Mdegella is also known as a leading *msanifu wa nyimbo*, composing in multiple musical styles. His musical compositions are his effort to blend personal theology with musical talent to express his belief in God. Mdegella does not compose music for contexts other than the church. His texts, most often taken directly from or inspired by the Bible, are inseparable in his mind from the melodies he assigns to them.

On several occasions Mdegella was asked about his approach to compositional method in order to understand of the process of conceptualization, development, and transmission of songs he engages:

GM: When I compose songs
there are times
that I do not
work it
myself
there are times when a song simply comes
to me
It moves
then I get it
and I write it down
but, there are times that I have to
look at Bible
get what I want to sing
then I start putting up music for
specifically for the
subjects
yeah
now, if
if my understanding of the Bible is
limited then definitely I
could also be very much limited in
what *I can possess*

"Putting up music," as Mdegella refers to the art of musical composition, is a process directly linked to the context of a song. In other words, there must be a *reason* for composing—a celebration, a request by another choir, a liturgy, a death, or a religious holiday.* As we sat together one day waiting for a choir rehearsal to start, Mdegella related the story of the origin of the *wimbo* ["song," singular of *nyimbo*], "Goodvoice and Victoria." On the occasion of the wedding of a member of *Kwaya ya Upendo*, Mdegella was asked to compose a special *wimbo*. He went home one night, wrote out a melody he had been thinking about all week, came back and taught the choir their new *wimbo* the following evening.

According to Mdegella, songs sometimes simply "came to him." It makes sense that Mdegella recognizes some form of divine contribution or involvement in his musical compositions, some way of linking his musical inspiration to divine or nonearthly power or authority. Mdegella followed up with the author concerning this issue of an intermediary connection between the divine and the human in musical composition, expanding on the mode of transmission of his thoughts, ideas, and inspirations to writing, harmonization, and finally to a choir.

AUTHOR: Last time we met you said "sometimes songs just come to me"

GM: And I'll repeat it again < >

AUTHOR: Where do they come from? Where does the inspiration *come from*?

GM: *Quiet moments*
that is one area where I do get
melodies flowing
quiet moments
sometimes, images
if someone is preaching
then I start
I start
thinking about what is being taught
I do have melodies flow
yes
and sometimes I do have dreams
you have that Easter cassette?

*In CD track 12, Mdegella responds my questions concerning the origins of style in contemporary compositions. As he explains, his African compositions "mix" and "twist" European and African sensibilities.

[hums a melody]
yeah, that one came to me

AUTHOR: It's a beautiful piece

GM: When I was in bed
yeah
I dreamt it
so I woke up
it was about
it was two in the night
I woke up and scribed it on the paper
I left it
went to bed
the next morning it was sung in the church

AUTHOR: < > That's wonderful

GM: Yeah
so that's how
quiet moments
or sometimes if I'm walking to the church
thinking about something
I reach somewhere
a melody comes
I think that this is the best we can do for this certain
event I stop there and write

Finding a quiet place where *nyimbo* come to him—in dreams, during walks, and even in the rushed moments of everyday living—allows Mdegella to "reach somewhere" and have melodies "flow." Mdegella's *nyimbo* have a high recognition factor; his compositional voice is distinctive. However, the identification of his compositions is not an issue for Mdegella:

AUTHOR: Why is it that whenever we sing a piece of yours in the choir I don't even have to ask if it's yours because I already know?

GM: Now, that is a point that several people have been talking aboutbut actually I consciously don't know that I'm intending to do something of my identity
I've been trying to avoid that

AUTHOR: That's very interesting
you don't hear something coming across as your voice?

GM: Yes

AUTHOR: But it's your voice

GM: I've been trying to avoid identities

AUTHOR: You can't avoid it

GM: So because maybe because I come from a tribe
I've been brought up there
now there are those
the rhythmic patterns of the music could sometimes be
now they could be explaining me
you know, somehow, what Hehe's built itself in my
mind about music
maybe they do display my origin yeah
but I sometimes try very much to avoid having that
that's why I do sometimes
take songs of other tribes
sometimes I take a Makonde song
or sometimes I take a Malawian song

Despite Mdegella's attempts to "avoid identities," his distinct compositional voice manages to come through. The melodic traditions and the "rhythmic patterns" of his ethnic group could very well "explain" Mdegella as he suggests.

CD track 13 is a recording of *Kwaya ya Upendo* rehearsing one of Mdegella's most respected compositions, " 'Sikiliza,' Asema Bwana" ["'Listen,' Says the Lord"], a *wimbo* sung by many choirs in Dar es Salaam. The opening section has a melodic figure similar to melodic figures of the WaNyamwezi people of central Tanzania. Mdegella pointed out several times that most Tanzanians would recognize this song as WaNyamwezi. The original KiSwahili text as well as an English translation follows.

" 'SIKILIZA,' ASEMA BWANA"
"Sikiliza," asema Bwana, watulizeni wenye uchungu
    "Listen," says the Lord, comfort those people with difficulties
Piga kelele utangazo kwa Yerusalem, kwamba vita vimekwisha
    Shout and proclaim this to Jerusalem, that the battle is over
Nimesikia "watulize watu wangu watulie"
    I have heard, "tell my people they should calm down"
Wamenililia basi wasilie watulie
    They have cried to me. Now they should no longer cry

"Sikiliza," asema Bwana, watulizeni wenye uchungu
"Listen," says the Lord, comfort those people with difficulties
Watulize mioyotaifa langu, tuwanyamazishe
My nation should be at ease, let us make quiet.
Ombolezo na kiliyo visisikike tena
Moaning and wailing should no longer be heard
Uovu nimefuta sitau kumbuka tena
I have forgiven the evils, I will not remember again
Mapigo wamepata yawatoshawatu wangu
The plagues that they have experienced are enough
Nitawatimizia agano langu la kale
And now I shall fulfill my ancient covenant
Atashuka kwambozi awaponye watu wangu
The Savior will descend to warn my people
Umefika ulemwaka wenye neema tele
The year has come that is full of grace
Yawajia Yerusalemu na ulimwengu wote
Which comes to Jerusalem and to the whole world
Tutauona wokovu wetu, Bwana umewaridhia watu
We shall see our salvation, which the Lord has given
Mwakozi yuaja watulizeni mioyo wote waliogizani
The Savior is coming, tell the people to be at ease
Nuru itawazukia wote
And the light will come over them
Tetema na kujifika tetema shetani atetema
Tremble and hide, tremble, the devil is trembling
Tetema na kujifika tetema duniani ishangilie
Tremble and hide, tremble, the world should rejoice
Tetema na kujifika tetema yuaja mwenye nguvu
Tremble and hide, tremble, the powerful one is coming
Tetema na kujifika tetema Mwana wake Mungu-hoyo
Tremble and hide, tremble, that is the Son of God
Tetema na kujifika tetema simba wa ukombozi
Tremble and hide, tremble, the lion of salvation

Other composer's songs are often simple, mimicking Western mission hymnody and easily "picked up" and memorized by a choir. Mdegella's compositions, however, can be somewhat complicated melodically and rhythmically, making it frustrating for him when a choir does not meet his standards.

As a self-trained composer, Mdegella is uncomfortable with attaching labels such as "African" or "European" to his musical compositions. In a discussion concerning musical *origins*, however, he readily agreed that music is inherently "culture bound." Understanding his compositions as either "Tanzanian" or "East African" music has become an important marker of distinction for Mdegella. To feel "at home," music must reflect the "social experience" of a people, community, or nation. For Mdegella, music is a marker not only of distinction, but also more importantly of a community's social identity:

> If you want to make something Tanzanian then you have to be Tanzanian. I don't just say this as my own opinion or principle. I'm trying to display the actual experience, the social experience people normally feel when they do things in their own way which identifies them and makes them feel more at home. We sometimes have these open-air Gospel evangelistic events. You won't hear German or English hymns there. No. We have what we call *mapambio*. They are like scriptures, we could rather call them scriptures or short, locally originated songs, which can easily be sung by everybody in their local melodies. Actually you see them more excited and they feel at home doing that. I wanted to say that through experience you will find that a society would like to present itself in its own terms.

ACTIVITY 4.1 *To approach the potential problem of* essentializing *East African cultures and musical specialists within those cultures, take the time to reflect on any reactions you might have to having your* culture, *your* community essentialized? *Essentializing usually refers to the process whereby a culture (a community, a group, or an individual) is reduced to its essence or an aspect of its intrinsic nature. For example, to label or identify all New Yorkers as rude and unfriendly is to essentialize an extremely large group of people based on behavioral patterns that do not translate across cultural communities—even across individuals.*

- Listen for one week for instances of essentializing about other people that you hear around you. Keep a record of them in writing, for discussion in class.
- Then consider this: Do your parents or relatives *essentialize* you according to your musical tastes, your CD collection, and your choice of radio station?

> • Do you, in turn, *essentialize* your parents' musical tastes, your fiends' musical tastes, and your roommates' tastes?

Mdegella and "First-Class Music."

Mdegella and I sit and visit together over another cup of tea. I can tell Mdegella is exhausted, more so than usual, and I leave soon after arranging to meet again the following day. As I am about to pack up my equipment, Mdegella touches my sleeve to get my attention. He slowly begins to tell me that he wants to answer an earlier question I raised about why he continues to invest so much time and energy with his compositions when he is currently enduring such severe economic hardships:

My music is about singing. I sing for God. I sing for my Lord. It's about Christian life—all my music. I've never composed outside, completely outside the Christian community. Really, I just want to *make first-class music.* That's all. After that I don't know what would be achieved. Maybe the simple desire of music. I'd be satisfied by having first-class music done by myself.

What does Mdegella want to accomplish musically? In this concluding passage he states that his primary goal is to compose "first-class music." In his songs, Mdegella reflects the many, critical historical changes that have occurred in Tanzania over the past forty years. He has been an active agent for change in contemporary music composition, and his *nyimbo* are consistently identified as a voice of the new, more *indigenized*, more African choir music tradition.

CENTURIO BALIKOOWA

I now shift to a narrative that focuses on another East African musician, Centurio Balikoowa, who lives and teaches in Kampala, the capital city of Uganda. This section begins by contextualizing his life so that, as Balikoowa once suggested to me, all students back home in America

FIGURE 4.2   *Photograph of Centurio Balikoowa.*   *(Photo by Gregory Barz.)*

will understand better how musicians who are trying to make their living in contemporary East Africa often live in *multiple musical worlds*.

In the sections that follow, the topic of "traditional" Ugandan music is introduced; for Balikoowa traditional music is that music that is still taught to, performed among, and embraced by rural-based ethnic groups. His point weaves neatly into organological descriptions of two important Ugandan instruments used in traditional music making, the *endere* (flute) and the *endingidi* (tubefiddle). After introducing aspects of traditional music Balikoowa's professional and personal history are addressed.

Background.   Centurio Balikoowa is one of the last students of the great performer and teacher of traditional Ugandan music, Evaristo Muyinda. For several generations Muyinda functioned as a portal of information about traditional Ugandan culture, teaching both local and foreign students (including foreign ethnomusicologists!). For many people Balikoowa now carries that torch, teaching both Ugandan students and foreign ethnographers. Balikoowa has functioned as the author's frequent research colleague and teacher, and he has toured the United States as a musician and as a teacher.

Balikoowa is strongly rooted in the rural, village-based musical traditions of Busoga in eastern Uganda (See Figure 1.1, for a map that includes Uganda), but he made the transition to urban life to pursue educational opportunities at an early age. His natural curiosity and musical aptitude led him to adopt a transnational musical repertory early in his career.

During one conversation with Balikoowa he was asked to address several of the critical issues that are raised throughout this textbook. The first was framed in the form of a question: *What is "traditional" Ugandan music?* Balikoowa's response:

Ugandan traditional music? Well, first of all I must mention that in Uganda we have different cultures, we have over thirty-two different languages, and out of those thirty-two languages we have different tribes, and each tribe has a different type of music. You'll find that every tribe has different rhythms, so in Ugandan music we have percussion instruments, we have string instruments, we have melodic instruments, and we have wind instruments, but they are played in an *African* way. So, *our* music is *of us* and *by us*, and it is therefore *traditional* music.

Even though Balikoowa identifies thirty-two different "music-languages," distinct musical "traditions," he maintains that there is something that can be called traditional "Ugandan" music:

I think we could say that each of those thirty-two different languages is *in* Uganda. But, the individual musical traditions that we play we consider "Ugandan" music. But in this region of Africa there are definite similarities in our music that we can easily identify. Even in the dances and costumes you can see similarities. There are some similarities in dance steps and in music also. For example, we have mainly five notes in the eastern part of Uganda. If you are from the western part of Uganda you will also have five notes. It is the *rhythm* that changes depending on where the music comes from.

Balikoowa notes that there is uniformity, such as in the use of scales—specifically the use of the pentatonic, five-note scale—among Ugandan traditions, but rhythms, such as those associated with particular traditional dances change from one ethnic group to another.

Musical Instruments.   There are a wide variety of instruments found in Ugandan cultures: aerophones (traditional flutes, panpipes), chordophones (string tubefiddles, harps, and lyres), membranophones (drums of all shapes and sizes grouped together or played individually), idiophones (melodic percussion rock chimes, plucked lamellophones, and xylophones). The type and variety of instruments depend on the region of the country. Xylophones and drums are virtually everywhere. Tubefiddles are also frequently found in many regions. A major characteristic highlighting the difference between East African musics and those of other sub-Saharan regions is a comfortable balance in East Africa between aerophones, chordophones, idiophones, and membranophones (see *Thinking Musically* for a discussion of organological categories). East Africa communities—perhaps more than other regions—use instruments to form unique ensembles, such as the *adungu* (arched or bow harp) ensembles of the Alur people, *akogo* (plucked lamellophones) ensembles of the Iteso people, the *endere* (notched-flute) ensembles of the Baganda people), among others. Ethnomusicologist Klaus Wachsmann's pioneering efforts, published as "The Sounding Instruments" (Wachsmann 1953) provides historical details of the beauty and unique qualities of many East African resources for the study of musical instruments as well as outlining characteristics that define regional similarities and variations.

Instruments are usually complemented by singing and dancing as well as clapping and ululation. Perhaps the most intriguing of all is the transformation of the human body into a musical instrument. In several parts of Uganda—but particularly in the west—rattles or bells are attached or wrapped around the lower legs of dancers (both male and female), transforming the body of a dancer into a rhythmicized, embodied musical instrument. In the energetic music and dances of the Ankole people, for example, dancers frequently jump and stamp their feet on the ground in highly rhythmic patterns, producing vivid sounding rhythms (see Figure 4.3).

Wherever one might find Balikoowa he is typically surrounded by musical instruments—in his classrooms in the Kibuli section of Kampala, in his home village of Kibaale-Busiki, when he comes to the USA to tour—musical instruments are everywhere. While several instruments in particular are closely associated with Balikoowa, above all he is considered one of the greatest *endere* (flute) players in Uganda today.

Endere (Flute).   There are two different types of notched *endere* (flutes)—one short and one long; all flutes in Uganda have four holes.

FIGURE 4.3   *Ankole dancer from Mbarara, Uganda, wearing rattles wrapped around his lower leg as he performs the* Runyege ngoma.   *(Photo by Gregory Barz.)*

Notched flutes are typically long tubes made from a variety of materials that have a square hole chipped out of one of the ends. It is through this notch that air is blown over, creating the sound on the flute. The short *endere* is typically found in the eastern part of Uganda where it is played among the Basoga people, and it is now often used only to accompany dancers, or just to entertain. The longer *endere* is typically found in the western part of the country among the Ankole people. Historically the *endere* was played as a solo instrument. Someone would sit down when bored and blow their flute, in the same way that they would take the *endingidi* (tubefiddle) and play alone. Only later did the *endere* join larger ensembles of different musical instruments. The *endere* was used at one time by shepherds to encourage cows to eat. Cows are thought to have listened to the blowing of the *endere* and in response graze from morning up until evening. The *endere* played in both western and eastern Uganda are now typically played to accompany the various traditional music performances of the region and to entertain people, and it is often played in combination with other instruments.

On CD track 14 Balikoowa demonstrates the pentatonic (five-note) tuning produced on the Ugandan *endere*. Even though there are only four holes, five notes are played as he demonstrates. On CD track 14 Balikoowa blows these five notes on both the large and small *endere*. Since the tuning of the *endere* is pentatonic, Balikoowa typically adapts the European solmization or "solfege" syllables in his Ugandan classroom (similar to the *embaire* example in Chapter 2). He leaves out "fa" and "ti" to approximate the tuning of the pentatonic scale used in Uganda.

Balikoowa outlines two different ways of understanding the tuning of the *endere* on CD track 14:

sol la do re mi   or   do re mi sol la
4   5   1   2 3   1   2   3   4   5

He first outlines an understanding of the tuning as existing in the middle of a continuum:

. . . do re mi sol la do re mi] [sol la do re mi] [sol la do re mi sol la . . .

He then outlines a unit that is a distinct group within this greater continuum:

[do re mi sol la]

Since the xylophone is omnipresent throughout Uganda (called *embaire* in eastern Uganda, *akadinda* or *amadinda* in central Uganda), the *endere* in any region would usually be tuned to a particular xylophone since notched flutes are easily made while the manufacture of xylophone keys is much more labor intensive. (*Note*: This is similar to other musico-cultural traditions, such as gamelan tuning systems in Indonesia.) Balikoowa demonstrates the eastern style of playing on the short *endere* in CD track 15. His *endere* is made from a sawed-off piece of plastic PVC pipe that has had holes bored into it with a manual drill, a typical modern method of manufacturing *endere*.

On CD track 16, Balikoowa plays the long *endere*, introducing an example from the western part of Uganda, specifically among the people called the BaNyankore (also "Nyankole" or "Ankole"). The BaNyankore are largely cattle keepers, and they play their *endere* while they look after their cows. Notice that the music played on this larger flute is a bit slower, reflecting for many the slower way people are thought to talk in the western regions. According to Balikoowa, the BaNyankore are a bit slow in their speech, while the Basoga in the east are a bit faster; the music therefore reflects this in his opinion. Other than tempo, the two styles are fundamentally similar.

The *endere* is such a strong symbol of Ugandan musical culture that one of the most important performing troupes specializing in traditional performances in the country has adopted the name of this instrument for their group, The Ndere Troupe in Kampala. Balikoowa was at one time the troupe's principal *endere* player.

Endingidi (Tubefiddle). The Ugandan one-string tubefiddle is called *endingidi* (Figure 4.4) (also frequently spelled *"ndingidi"* for linguistic reasons). The one-string *endingidi* chordophone is played on the hip or side of the body rather than rested on the shoulder, such as with the violin, and is tuned to whatever instrument it accompanies. The *endingidi* uses the same pentatonic scale as the *endere*, as Balikoowa demonstrates on CD track 17.

On CD track 18 you will hear Balikoowa and the author playing a medley of tunes together on two *endingidi* tuned to the same open-string pitch. The first piece in the medley is *"Adimudong',"* a song from the northern part of Uganda. The second piece is "Twalamatagange" from the western part of Uganda, and the third piece is a melody from the central region of the country.

FIGURE 4.4 *Photograph of an* Endingidi. *(Photo by Gregory Barz.)*

Endingidi can, however, be tuned to different pitches; three *endingidi* can play together, for example, with three different tunings. Players in this type of three-part tuning style assume different roles, often according to the size of the *endingidi*: small, medium, and large:

Lutamba	the leading part (largest *endingidi*)
Katamba	the secondary player (smallest *endingidi*)
Kitamba	the third, supporting player (medium *endingidi*)

When there is an ensemble of three *endingidi*, two play in contrasting keys, while the third player is expected to improvise and "color" the original melody.

Ornamentation—or the elaboration on a given melodic idea—is extremely important in Ugandan music. In most Uganda musics there is an expectation that music will *always* be developed within performance. Melodies are considered boring if fresh, new ideas are not continually added into performance. Balikoowa refers to ornamentation as a way of "coloring" improvised music. He feels that if he plays music "straight" then he will bore people (and himself), and that the very soul of a melody (its meaning and its true character) is revealed only when it is ornamented within improvisation. On CD track 19, Balikoowa demonstrates ornamental improvisation of a "straight" melody juxtaposed to a "colored" melody. In this example Balikoowa *develops* or "colors" the same melody in different ways.

Construction of the **Endingidi.** The *endingidi* is made up of several detachable parts (see Figure 4.5), and can therefore be easily dismantled and carried around. The instrument's string was traditionally made of sisal, a fiber manufactured from the sisal plant grown throughout East Africa. This sisal fiber is also used for the hair of the *endingidi* bow. Problematic due to constant breaking, sisal has largely been replaced by the introduction of monofilament nylon strings, similar to fishing line cord. The newer nylon (and occasionally, wire) strings also provide *endingidi* players with greater opportunities for amplification, allowing them to be heard within larger ensembles. The instrument's sound box is made from a hollowed piece of wood from the *settaala* tree which yields a soft wood. Another wood that is sometimes used is called *musambya*, a harder wood more typically used to make xylophone keys. The skin from a monitor lizard (or young goat or cow) is placed over the sound box of the *endingidi*. (The skin of older cows is hard and not as pliant as that of younger animals and if used will not vibrate properly.) The skin is first placed in water until it becomes soft; it is then

FIGURE 4.5 *Photograph of Gayira playing the 8-string ntongooli.* *(Photo by Gregory Barz.)*

placed over the sound box, tied over the open hole and hammered into place with holding pegs. When the skin dries it becomes firm and it remains in place. The instrument's handle is carved from the wood of any hard tree, as is the tuning peg, which is added to adjust the pitch of the string.

The animal hair typically placed at the top of the instrument is merely for decoration. The *endingidi* was at one time meant to be played before local kings who would gather good musicians for entertainment purposes at their courts. These musicians felt that their village instruments were overly bare and not complete, and in response they added the ornamentation of a goat's tail or a cow's tail on the top for decoration. The bow that is drawn across the *endingidi's* string originated with hunting, according to Balikoowa, and while many players continue to use sisal for their bows, others now use metal wire, which produces a much louder sound on the instrument. The *endingidi* also has a bridge to enable more sound to resonate. These bridges are made from soft papyrus or from the stem of corn plants after they have been dried.

    Endingidi are still made by hand in villages and can take anywhere from five to six months to complete. The carving of the wood is the initial step. It must be left to dry several times, after which the carving process is repeated. After the skin is placed on the body of the tube-fiddle it is again left to dry for several days. All *endingidi* are still made in this traditional way by hand; none are the product of industrial manufacture.

Ntongooli *(Bowl Lyre).*   The final musical instrument introduced is the eight-string *ntongooli* (bowl lyre). (Depending on the area of the country, this instrument may also be referred to as *ndongo, edungu,* or *litungu.*) The *ntongooli* is another instrument closely associated with Ugandan traditional musician Centurio Balikoowa. Both his father and grandfather were recognized players of the *ntongooli,* and Balikoowa has been featured on several recordings and documentary videos singing and playing the *ntongooli.* There are two contemporary types of lyres existing in sub-Saharan Africa today—box lyres and bowl lyres. There remains only one box lyre currently used in this area of the world, the *beganna* of the Amhara people of the East African countries of Eritrea and Ethiopia. This is the reason for referring to the *ntongooli* as a "bowl" lyre rather than just a "lyre."

    The *ntongooli* is a virtuosic instrument typically played as a solo instrument by the country's greatest artists, such as Evaristo Muyinda, Balikoowa, ethnomusicologists James Makubuya and Sylvia Tamusuza, and the young, upcoming artist Kitogo George Ndugwa. Figure 4.5 is a photograph of Gayira, one of the last, great drum-makers associated with the Buganda royal court, as he plays an *endongo*—a Baganda form of the Basoga *ntongooli*—he made for the author.

    On CD track 20 you will hear Balikoowa demonstrate a mnemonic device, a series of words in the Luganda language of the Baganda people used by *ntongooli/endongo* players to remember the intervallic pitch relationships used for tuning the instrument. He plucks the strings in consecutive order from left to right on the *ntongooli/endongo* (see Gayira in Figure 4.6 doing just this) to demonstrate the tuning. As he plucks,

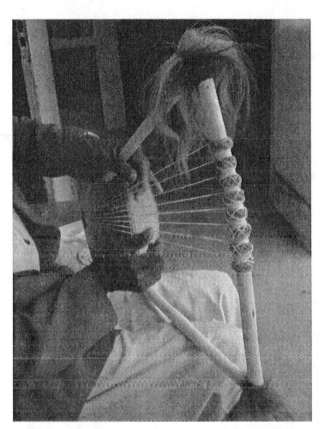

FIGURE 4.6 *Close-up of Gayira playing the 8-string* ntonghooli. *(Photo by Gregory Barz.)*

Balikoowa assigns a series of syllables to the notes, introducing the phrase, "Lwa lero wafe baase nte," which he translates into English as "At our home there they've killed a cow."

Luganda	Lwa	le-	ro	wa-	fe	baa-	se	nte
English	At	our	home	there	they've	killed	a	cow

On CD track 21 Balikoowa demonstrates the incredible virtuosity demanded of *ntongooli* players. He sings in his local language, Lusoga. (For an expanded study of the *ntongooli/endongo* see Makubuya 1995.)

ACTIVITY 4.2   *The final audio example in this chapter—CD track 22—demonstrates how music can be played on different instruments. You will hear a recording of "Twalamatagange" played by Centurio Balikoowa on the* ntongooli *accompanied by Kiria Moses on the* endingidi. *"Twalamatagange" was originally introduced on CD track 18 as part of an* endingidi *medley. Note the differences in style when played on the* ntongooli. *Attempt to articulate the differences that occur when the melody of "Twalamatagange" is played on a single string instrument* (endingidi) *from when it is played on a multistring instrument* (ntongooli).

Personal History.   Music was everywhere in the village within which Balikoowa grew up. He began his musical education by playing musical games when only three years old. His grandfather played a *ntongooli* bowl lyre and passed along the tradition to Balikoowa's father. He eventually learned to play the *ntongooli* himself by observing his father, just as his father has learned by observing his grandfather. He learned to play the *embaire* (xylophone) at an early age; almost all children in his village played homemade *embaire* with five wooden keys. Balikoowa remembers hearing someone playing a *endere* (flute) as they took care of the neighboring grazing cows, and he notes that he was able to play the same melodies he heard performed by shepherds the next time he grazed his own cow.

The *embaire* is an important aspect of memories of his village culture. Every evening as people came home from working in the fields, they made their way through his village where there was no electricity. Instead of going home to watch television or rent a video, adults typically worked together to construct the village's *embaire* and then take turns playing it through the night. Once an evening's music making heated up, the sounds of the *embaire* could often be heard in neighboring villages where residents responded by contributing their own performances to the evening soundscape. Such competitive music making would often continue through the night. Most people normally started to play music in such contexts when they were still young. Balikoowa started by imitating his parents. Music is typically passed along this way, through imitation and repetition.

Neither his parents nor family of village farmers were in a position to pay Balikoowa's school fees, a required expense to finance children's education in Uganda in the era before U.P.E. (universal primary education). While he was in first grade he had begun to play the *ntongooli* (bowl lyre), and by several accounts those who listened to him were amazed. The principal of his primary school recognized his musical abilities and offered him a scholarship that enabled him to continue his education. In school, he found that he could pass along his musical knowledge to his fellow students: how to play the instruments, how to arrange them in groups, and how to compose new songs and pieces based on village traditions. Thus, he assumed the role of teacher as well as student very early in life.

After seventh grade Ugandan children typically progress to secondary school. At this point in Balikoowa's education, adjudicators came from the nation's capitol to observe the annual music festivals of Balikoowa's home region in Busoga. They quickly noticed Balikoowa playing the *endere, ntongooli, endingidi*, and *embaire*. At one performance he surrounded himself with five instruments and played them all to the astonishment of the visitors. One of the adjudicators, a teacher from Makerere College, a secondary school affiliated with Makerere University in Kampala, observed him and offered him a scholarship on the spot to continue his studies in the capital.

Balikoowa learned most of his music repertoire that is not based on his village's traditions from Evaristo Muyinda, a former musician in the royal Buganda court who went on to become an internationally famous performer and teacher. When Balikoowa moved to Kampala, the capital city of Uganda, from his home area, Busoga, he began learning musical traditions from throughout the country under Muyinda's tutelage. As a teenager he found himself living within a different ethnic group— the Baganda people—from whom he grew up, and who had a somewhat different music tradition, albeit at some level based on very old Basoga traditional dance and music. Balikoowa recalls that at the time he was in school the only way to make a living as a musician was to become a teacher, and so he eventually joined a TTC (Teacher's Training College).

After his teaching degree program he assumed a position as a music teacher at the local Police Children School in Kampala where he works to this day with students, many of whom have not had the opportunity to learn the traditions of their parents' home villages. Many of his students experience and learn traditional Ugandan music for the first time in his classes. Children therefore learn traditional music and dance in elementary schools today, while others continue to learn the traditions of their culture and community in their home village communities.

ACTIVITY 4.3 *Gideon Mdegella and Centurio Balikoowa represent musical specialists, empowered individuals in their communities, in unique ways. Write a brief essay, to relate this to your own experience.*

- Are musical specialists assigned, appointed, or remunerated for their efforts in your own world, in your own culture, in your own community, in your own family?
- In what ways—if any—are the musical specialists with whom you are most familiar similar to Mdegella and Balikoowa?
- In what ways are they different?

CONCLUSION

This chapter opened with two epigraphs in which both Gideon Mdegella and Centurio Balikoowa state rather emphatically their need to make music: "I make music because I must," according to Mdegella, and "I play because I must play," according to Balikoowa. The multiple cultural systems from which these two musicians emerge play important roles in both forming the contexts of these artists' efforts as well as informing the creativity that allows these individuals efforts to flourish. Mdegella and Balikoowa engage the trajectory of rural and urban experiences that are very present in East African cultures to a significant degree in their musical compositions, teaching, and performances. Moving across boundaries where electricity lines start and stop is normative for these musicians (as it is for most others in this area of the world), and the efforts of Mdegella and Balikoowa (and countless others) represent local responses to the transmission of traditional musical cultures in East Africa.

CHAPTER 5

Situating Traditional Music within Modernity

INTRODUCTION

Contact with other cultures (both neighboring and foreign) is nowhere more significantly expressed in East Africa than in contemporary, urban performances of music, dance, and drama. At present, traditional and indigenous musical, religious, and linguistic systems coexist within soundscapes sharing inherited and external systems in many parts of this geographic region. *The maintenance of traditional forms of music—and music in general—must be understood as a critical response to shifts of identity, often in response to contact with modernity.*

Several layers of roots that feed life into popular music traditions in East Africa are engaged in this chapter by presenting popular and traditional elements of expressive culture as inherently interdependent. Traditional musical materials are drawn on to present both new musical forms and reinvented traditions for such popular traditions. *Benga,* for example, is presented in this chapter as an example in which the traditional roots of the Luo praise-singing style of *nyatiti* performance are maintained while simultaneously presenting a form that challenges the boundaries of traditional and popular.

This chapter outlines two specific ways in which traditional performance and traditional culture today intersect with the commercialization of popular and artistic culture in this region of the world. Ugandan composer Justinian Tamusuza's string quartet "Mu Kkubo Ery 'Omusaalaba" challenges the players as well as us, the audience, to engage the melodic and rhythmic *kiganda* materials on multiple levels. These levels suggest that Tamusuza is a contemporary Ugandan composer comfortable living within and communicating to multiple musical worlds—African and non-African. His string quartet functions as a musical bridge connecting his ever-expanding worldviews with those of audiences at home and abroad. In this way Tamusuza's string quartet is a strong and significant response to modernity in East Africa. "Jo Piny," a signature piece for Kenya's Kabila Klan demonstrates that *benga* continues to be maintained and preserved as an older guitar-band tradition in western Kenya and has influenced other emergent popular music forms, while at the same time referencing traditional Luo *nyatiti* praise-singing.

Documenting, understanding, and representing African popular culture of the past century is of increasing importance to students, historians, ethnomusicologists, and the recording industry. Yet as ethnomusicologist Gerhard Kubik suggests, "historical consciousness remains low in the general African public. Mid-twentieth century styles are quickly dismissed as 'out-of-date' or 'colonial' by youths" (Kubik 2000:207). While it is true that music traditions in Africa have changed dramatically in the past fifty years, understanding how many traditional and popular contexts join together and affect each other in the modern world to produce contemporary music can only add to our appreciation and understanding of music in East Africa.

In the vignette that follows, the layers of identity that exist within many contemporary East African communities are revealed as modernity is negotiated in an urban context.

VIGNETTE: ANTHEMS AND IDENTITY

Excerpt from Fieldnotes. *I arrive in the early afternoon at the Makerere College School in Kampala, the capital city of Uganda, to discuss issues related to the use of music, dance, and drama in HIV/AIDS sensitization efforts with a group of secondary school students. The group requests that we begin our session by singing the country's national anthem. We quickly arrange ourselves as if forming a choir, assuring that each voice part in the anthem's four-part harmony will be covered (I join the tenor section). After some negotiation several boys are "made into sopranos" to make up for a lack of girls, and we begin the anthem.*

 The first two verses of the national anthem of Uganda can be heard at the beginning of the medley included on CD track 23. The complete text (three verses) and the score for the anthem in staff notation follow.

OLUYIMBA LW'EGGWANGA (EBBONA LYA AFIRIKA)
[THE PEARL OF AFRICA]

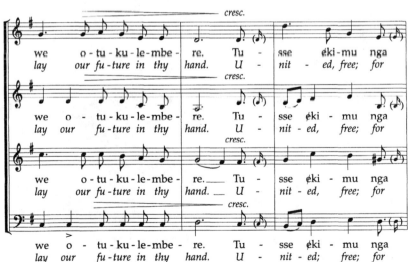

FIGURE 5.1 Score—Ugandan National Anthem, "Oluyimba Lw'eggwanga (Ebbona lya Afirika)" ["The Pearl of Africa"]. *(Music and English text by George W. Kakoma; Luganda translation by Busuulwa Katambula.)*

(continued)

tu - li mu ki-si-nde ky'e-mi - re - mbe.
li - ber-ty To-geth-er we'll al - ways stand.

tu - li mu ki-si-nde ky'e-mi - re - mbe.
li - ber - ty To-geth-er we'll al - ways stand.

tu - li mu ki-si-nde ky'e-mi - re - mbe.
li - ber - ty To-geth-er we'll al - ways stand.

tu - li mu ki-si-nde ky'e-mi - re - mbe.
li - ber - ty To-geth-er we'll al - ways stand.

Verse 1

Ggwe Uganda! Dolunda akunyweze
  Oh Uganda! May God uphold thee
Naawe otukulembere
  We lay our future in thy hand
Tusse ekimunga tulimu
  United, free; For liberty
Kisinde ky'emirembe.
  Together we'll always stand.

Verse 2

Ggwe Uganda! Ensi ey'eddembe
  Oh Uganda! The land of freedom

FIGURE 5.1 *Continued*

Wamma ka tukuweereze
  Our love and labor we give
Nga (twa)galena nnyo ne bannaffe
  And with neighbors all, at our country's call
Baliranwa bo bonna.
  In peace and friendship we'll live.

Verse 3
Ggwe Uganda atweyagaza
  Oh Uganda! The land that feeds us
Lw'obugimu n'akasana
  By sun and fertile soil grown
Ffe abaana bo tunaataasanga
  For our own dear land we'll always stand
Ensi ehhona ly'Afrika.
  The pearl of Africa's crown.

FIGURE 5.1   *Continued*

Excerpt from Fieldnotes. I thank the group of school youth as we finish singing the national anthem and assume that we will now proceed to the issues I have come prepared to address. Before I can begin, however, one of the students, Kitogo George Ndugwa, stops me, suggesting that it is appropriate that the group should now sing the anthem of the Buganda kingdom, since the school is located in the heart of the area populated by the Baganda ethnic group.

The first two verses of "Ekitibwa kya Buganda" ["The Pride of Buganda"], the anthem of the Baganda people, can be heard at 0:35 on CD track 23. The complete text (five verses) and the score in staff notation follow.

Verse 1

Okuva edda n'edda eryo lyonna
    Since time immemorial, years ago
Lino eggwanga Buganda
    This tribe of Buganda
Anti lyamanyibwa nnyo Eggwanga lyaffe
    It became famous this tribe of ours
Okwetooloola Ensi yonna
    So, let us love our tribe

Chorus

Twesiimye nnyo, Twesiimye nnyo
    We are proud, We are proud

FIGURE 5.2   *Score—Buganda Anthem, "Ekitiibwa kya Buganda" ["The Pride of Buganda"].   (Music and text by Reverend Polycarp Kakooza.)*

(continued)

Chorus

Olwa Buganda yaffe
   Because of our Buganda
Ekitiibwa kya Buganda kyava dda
   Great Buganda started long ago and will always be great
Naffe tukikuume nga
   Let us uphold the greatness of Buganda

Verse 2
Abazira ennyo abaatusooka
   The heroes who came before us
Baalwana nnyo mu ntalo
   They fought in so many wars
Ne balyagala nnyo Eggwanga lyaffe
   And they loved our kingdom so much
Naffe tulyagalenga
   So we too should love it

FIGURE 5.2   *Continued*

Verse 3
Ffe abaana ba leero ka tulwane
  So, we the new generation, let us try our best
Okukuza Buganda
  To develop Buganda
Nga tujjukira nnyo Bajjajja baffe
  While remembering our great grandparents
Abafiirira Ensi yaffe
  They died for the good of our kingdom

Verse 4
Nze nnaayimba nrya ne sitenda
  How can I sing and not praise
Ssaabasajja Kabaka
  His Highness the Kabaka (king)
Assanira afuge Obuganda bwonna
  He is fit to rule the whole kingdom of Buganda
Naffee nga tumwesiga
  And we must trust him

Verse 5
Katonda omulungi ow'ekisa
  Oh God, Lord who has mercy
Otubeere Mukama
  Have mercy on us, oh Lord
Otubundugguleko emikisa gyo era
  Bless us oh Lord with all your blessings
Bbaffe omukuumenga
  Give long-lasting life to our king and protect him

"EKITIIBWA KYA BUGANDA"
Lwayiiyizibwa Rev. Polycarp Kakooza (amaloboozi n'ebigambo) mu
1939, n'alukyusaamu katono mu 1990

$$
\left\{
\begin{array}{l}
\text{s,} \quad |\text{m} \qquad :\text{m.m} \quad |\text{m} \qquad :\text{r.d} \quad |l,:\text{-} \quad |\text{d} :\text{-} \quad \|\text{s} :\text{-} \quad .\text{s} \qquad \|\text{l.s} : \text{d.m} \quad |\text{r} :\text{-}|\text{-}:\text{-}.\| \\
\text{s,} \quad |\text{d} \qquad :\text{d.d} \quad |\text{d} \qquad :.\text{s,.s} \quad |\text{f,:-} \quad |\text{f} :\text{-} \quad \|\text{s,} :\text{-} \quad .\text{d} \qquad |\text{d.d} : \text{d.d} \quad |\text{t,} :\text{-}|\text{-}:\text{-}.\| \\
\text{s,} \quad |\text{s} \qquad :\text{s.s} \quad |\text{s} \qquad :\text{f.m} \quad |\text{d}:\text{-} \quad |\text{f} :\text{-} \quad \|\text{m} :\text{-} \quad .\text{m} \qquad |\text{f.m} : \text{s.s} \quad |\text{s} :\text{-}|\text{-}:\text{-}.\| \\
\text{s,} \quad |\text{d} \qquad :\text{d.d} \quad |\text{d} \qquad :\text{r,.m,} \quad |\text{f,:-} \quad |\text{d,} :\text{-} \quad \|\text{d} :\text{-} \quad .\text{d} \qquad |\text{d.d} : \text{d.d} \quad |\text{s,} :\text{-}|\text{-}:\text{-}.\|
\end{array}
\right\}
$$

FIGURE 5.2   *Continued*

$$
\left\{
\begin{array}{l}
\text{s,} \quad |\text{m.m : m.m} \quad |\text{m.d : r.d} \quad \|\text{l, :- } \quad |\text{d :- l,} \quad \| \text{.s, : r.m} \quad \text{f : } \quad \text{t,} \quad |\text{d :-|-:-.}\| \\
\text{s,} \quad |\text{d.d : d.d} \quad |\text{d.s, : .s,.s,} \quad |\text{f, :- } \quad |\text{l, :- f,} \quad \| \text{m, : .s,s,} \quad \text{s, : } \quad \text{s,} \quad |\text{s, :-|-:-.} \\
\text{s,} \quad |\text{s.s : s.s} \quad |\text{s.m : f.m} \quad |\text{d :- } \quad |\text{d :- d} \quad \| \text{d : m.f} \quad \text{s : } \quad \text{f} \quad |\text{m :-|-:-.} \\
\text{s,} \quad |\text{d.d : d.d} \quad |\text{d.d : r.m} \quad |\text{f, :- } \quad |\text{f, :- f,} \quad \| \text{s, : .s,.s,} \quad \text{s, : } \quad \text{s,} \quad |\text{d, :-|-:-.}\|
\end{array}
\right\}
$$

CHORUS

$$
\left\{
\begin{array}{l}
|\text{m : m.m} \quad |\text{m :- } |\text{d} \quad \text{d..d} \quad |\text{d :- } \|\text{l, : } \quad \text{l,l,} \quad |\text{s, : d} \quad |\text{r :-|- }\|\text{:s,} \quad .\text{s,} \\
|\text{d : d.d} \quad |\text{d :- } |\text{s,} \quad .\text{s,..s,} \quad |\text{s, :- } \|\text{f, : } \quad \text{f,f,} \quad |\text{m, : s,} \quad |\text{s, :-|- }\|\text{:s,} \quad \text{s,} \\
|\text{s : s.s} \quad |\text{s :- } |\text{m} \quad \text{m,m,} \quad |\text{m :- } \|\text{d : } \quad \text{d,d,} \quad |\text{d : d} \quad |\text{t, :-|- }\|\text{:s,} \quad .\text{s.} \\
|\text{d : d.d} \quad |\text{d :- } |\text{d,} \quad \text{d,d,} \quad |\text{d, :- } \|\text{f, : } \quad \text{f,f,} \quad |\text{d, : m,} \quad |\text{s, :-|- }\|\text{:s,} \quad .\text{s,}
\end{array}
\right\}
$$

$$
\left\{
\begin{array}{l}
|\text{m} \quad .\text{m : } \quad \text{m.} \quad |\text{m}|\text{m : r} \quad .\text{d} \quad \|\text{l, :- } \quad |\text{d _. l} \quad \|\text{s : r} \quad \text{m}|\text{f : t,} \quad |\text{d :- -:-.} \\
|\text{d} \quad \text{d : } \quad \text{d.} \quad |\text{d}|\text{d : .s,} \quad .\text{s,} \quad |\text{f, :- } \quad \text{l, _. f,} \quad \|\text{m, : s,} \quad \text{s,}|\text{s, : s,} \quad |\text{s :- -:-.} \\
|\text{s} \quad .\text{s : } \quad \text{s.} \quad |\text{s}|\text{s : f} \quad .\text{m} \quad |\text{d :- } \quad |\text{d _. d} \quad \|\text{d : d} \quad \text{m}|\text{s, : f} \quad |\text{m :- -:-.} \\
|\text{d} \quad .\text{d : } \quad \text{d.} \quad |\text{d}|\text{d : r,} \quad .\text{m,} \quad |\text{f, :- } \quad \text{f, _. f,} \quad \|\text{m, : .s,} \quad \text{s,}|\text{s, : s,} \quad |\text{d :- -:-.}
\end{array}
\right\}
$$

FIGURE 5.2 *Continued*

Excerpt from Fieldnotes. *After five verses of the rousing Buganda anthem I again ready myself with a set of questionnaires until Kitogo George Ndugwa again stops me, asking if it would be all right if the group of students now sang their house anthem, as all of the assembled students are associated with one particular campus house, Africa House.*

The first verse of "Marching Along," Africa House's anthem, can be heard at 1:20 on CD track 23. The complete text (three verses) and the score in staff notation follow.

"MARCHING ALONG," AFRICA HOUSE ANTHEM

Chorus

*We young women and men of Uganda are marching along the path of
    education*
Singing and dancing with joy together, uniting for a better Uganda.

Verse 1

*We are the pillars of tomorrow's Uganda, let's rise now, embrace true
    knowledge*
Yielding discipline, resourcefulness to rebuild the great, great pearl.

FIGURE 5.3 *Africa House Anthem, "Marching Along."* (Melody and words by
Arthur W. Musulube; harmonization by J. Hobday.)

(continued)

Verse 2
We know the way into the land of enlightenment has thorns, creepers,
   vales, and mountains
Come what may we shall overcome, for the glorious times to come.

Verse 3
Parents and teachers and the youths of this nation rise with us, support our
   endeavors
Led by God, who is the source of life, to uplift our motherland.

FIGURE 5.3   Continued

For most people in contemporary East Africa numerous interdependent political, geo-cultural, and social issues related to modernity contribute to the formation of individual and collective identity. The singing of anthems as a cultural frame of reference detailed in the lyrics offered by the secondary school youth at Makerere College School introduces this wonderfully complicated relationship between identity and modernity as a distinctly musical process. The medley on CD track 23 demonstrates how issues of identity are represented to the youth themselves—that is a sense of nation (by singing the Ugandan national anthem first), a sense of tribe or ethnic group (by singing the Buganda anthem), and a sense of community (by singing the anthem associated with Africa House). And perhaps most significant in this musical gesture is the purposeful coupling of the three aspects of identity together in these songs.

This fifth chapter illustrates in detail two ways in which modernity in East Africa is expressed through self and collective identity. Before launching this chapter's first case study, however, a general definition of "modernity" is offered from the most recent edition of the *Oxford English Dictionary:*

> *Modernity*—An intellectual tendency or social perspective characterized by departure from or repudiation of traditional ideas, doctrines, and cultural values in favour of contemporary or radical values and beliefs (chiefly those of scientific rationalism and liberalism).

The two case studies presented next will appear to call into question the monodirectionality of this conceptualization of modernity (perhaps biased by Western notions of rationalism). It should in fact become clear that while there is "departure" and perhaps even "repudiation" of traditional culture in the example, there is also a level of retention of older "ideas, doctrines, and cultural values" within musical performances of "modern" values and beliefs.

In many ways identity formation in East Africa embraces *both* Western and indigenous African musical aesthetics—"departing" yet retaining, "repudiating" while simultaneously preserving. The contemporary examples will demonstrate specific ways in which popular musics and new art music forms often have their historical roots within traditional performance. The case studies provided in this chapter also demonstrate ways in which contemporary musics interact with other outside musical cultures in response to colonization, missionization, commercialism, and nationalism.

CASE STUDY #1: "MU KKUBO ERY 'OMUSAALABA"

"Mu Kkubo Ery 'Omusaalaba" or "On the Way of the Cross" is a string quartet, a major musical work by the Ugandan composer Justinian Tamusuza. The compositions of Tamusuza purposefully blend European and Ugandan musical sensibilities, drawing both on the composer's African roots and his European and American compositional training. In response to a comment once made by the author questioning how it could be otherwise for composers trained as he was, Tamusuza's response is telling—"Why should it be otherwise?" he posited. By drawing on hymn tunes the composer demonstrates influences of missionization and colonization in "Mu Kkubo Ery 'Omusaalaba". Recognized as a leading contemporary African composer, Tamusuza has written a number of chamber and solo works for musicians trained in the European tradition that incorporate traditional African melodies, harmonics, polyrhythms, and other musical sensibilities. Several of his works demonstrate his familiarity with minimalist techniques, emphasizing the repetition of simple melodic lines, harmonic progression, and rhythmic patterns. The string quartet "Mu Kkubo Ery 'Omusaalaba," however, draws heavily on the musical traditions of the Baganda people of Buganda in central Uganda.

Born in 1951 in Kibisi, Uganda, Tamusuza's early musical training was in the singing, drumming, and *endingidi* (tubefiddle) playing typical of *kiganda* traditional music (*kiganda* is the adjectival form used to refer to expressive culture of the Baganda people). Tamusuza's father was known for brewing a form of local beer that attracted many people to his family's homestead. It was at these gatherings while still a child that Tamusuza typically heard local musical traditions performed for him and his family. He first studied musical composition with Anthony Okelo in Uganda and later with Kevin Volans at Queens University in Belfast, ultimately receiving the doctorate in musical composition at Northwestern University in the United States. Tamusuza lives and teaches in Kampala, Uganda where he is a professor and the former head of the department of Music, Dance, and Drama at Makerere University.

Tamusuza came to world attention through the Kronos Quartet, whose recording *Pieces of Africa* featured a movement of Tamusuza's first string quartet. By many accounts Tamusuza's composition is the most lively and appreciated on the album. The recording reached No. 1 on both the Billboard Classical *and* World Music Charts in 1992.

Tamusuza has since been inundated with commissions from major artists and ensembles throughout the world.

Basic Tenets of Kiganda Traditional Music. The central kingdom of Buganda, Tamusuza's home, lies on the northern shore of Lake Victoria to the west of the source of the Nile River in the country of Uganda (refer to the map given as Figure 1.1). Instrumentalists affiliated with the Buganda royal court included famous ensembles of drummers, side-blown trumpets, xylophones, flutes, and panpipes. The famous and large *akadinda* (xylophone) with up to 22 free keys was the exclusive instrument of the Buganda *kabaka* (king), the same royal court for which *Baakisimba* was created (refer to the first chapter for further information about *Baakisimba*). Yet, the music of the Baganda royal courts has long been inseparable from everyday traditional musical performances of the Baganda people.

Buganda   Central Ugandan kingdom
Baganda   The people of Buganda
Kiganda   Adjectival form of Baganda, pronounced "chi-GAH-nda"

Tamusuza's composition, "Mu Kkubo Ery 'Omusaalaba," often relies on the imitation and evocation of Ugandan instruments such as the *endingidi* (tubefiddle) and the *akadinda* (xylophone) in addition to the simulation of *kiganda* musical aesthetics. To perform this string quartet Western-trained players often have to rethink their techniques and their approach to their Western string instruments. Several of the basic tenets of *kiganda* music will now be introduced.

Issue of Timbre. The first *kiganda* aesthetic issue that will be explored is *timbre*, particularly the *sound* of traditional *kiganda* string music. The issue of timbre is clearly highlighted in many parts of Tamusuza's string quartet. On CD track 24 you will hear a brief demonstration of the typical playing style of the *kiganda* one-string *endingidi* (tubefiddle, chordophone) of the Baganda people that was discussed in detail in the previous chapter. This recorded example communicates something of the timbre—the raspy, dry timbre typically associated with the *kiganda* *endingidi* and reminds us of the examples demonstrated in Chapter 4.

As you listen to CD track 24 played on an *endingidi* you might be able to detect words such as "America" and "London." The performer, Kiria Moses, suggests that even if you are from America and London you will be able to enjoy this piece. Tamusuza imitates the timbre produced on the *endingidi* clearly in the score of his string quartet (Figure 5.4).

Mu Kkubo Ery' Omusalaaba
Ekitundu Ekisooka

FIGURE 5.4 *Example from the score of "Mu Kkubo Ery 'Omusaalaba."*

FIGURE 5.5   *Photograph of the Blair String Quartet (Felix Wang, John Kochanowski, Christian Teal, and Cornelia Heard).   (Used by permission of Vanderbilt University.)*

This subtle timbre is produced by the marking *sul ponticello,* an indication instructing the string quartet players to place their bows close to the bridge of their instruments. This creative technique evokes the raspy sound of the *endingidi.* Tamusuza's intent is to map the timbre of *kiganda* string playing onto this performance of a Western string quartet. The passage shown in Figure 5.4 can be heard on CD track 25 as the American group, the Blair String Quartet affects the timbre of the *endingidi* (Figure 5.5).

Drumming.   Another tenet of traditional *kiganda* music evoked in Tamusuza's score is a reliance on drumming. Drumming in both royal and village contexts in Buganda is perhaps the most conspicuous aspect of *kiganda* music. Particular drums are often prescribed for specific performance events. For example, traditional wrestling matches require drumming on a specific drum called the *engalabi,* a tall, single headed drum with a monitor lizard-skin head (Figure 5.6); this drum is struck with bare hand. The sound of the *engalabi* is crisp and clear, and it is indispensable to many important social occasions, such as funeral rites in which elders appoint successors to the deceased.

FIGURE 5.6 *Photograph of* baakisimba *drum.* *(Photo by Jonathan Rogers.)*

CD track 26 depicts a particular *kiganda* rhythm that is played on the *baakisimba* drum. The author plays the rhythm as it was first taught to him by the Ugandan musician Albert Bisaso. This rhythm is specifically associated with the royal *kiganda* music dance known as *Baakisimba* detailed in the first chapter of this volume. The *baakisimba* drum gets its name from its prominent use and role in *Baakisimba*. As the author plays, notice the particular sound, the timbre that is produced on the very large drumhead.

Evoking rhythmic patterns associated with the sounds of drums is particularly highlighted in Tamusuza's string quartet as the players are required to produce such patterns directly on their instruments. The drumming of intricate rhythms on the bodies of musical instruments is also a common feature in his composition. While the original score for "Mu Kkubo Ery 'Omusaalaba" indicates that the rhythmic patterns should be performed on the instruments of the string quartet themselves, players faced with performing in larger halls and auditoriums typically substitute drums, as is the case with the Blair String Quartet in CD track 27. They also use drums and rattles (prescribed in Tamusuza's score) to evoke the rhythmic interplay of traditional *kiganda* drumming.

Issue of Interlocking Patterns. The third and final tenet of typical *kiganda* tradition music that will be highlighted in this chapter is that of interlocking patterns. Instrumental music that is presented in several unique yet interdependent parts dominates *kiganda* music, and the successive entry of parts, of melodic ideas is a characteristic feature. Justinian Tamusuza suggested to the author that *kiganda* melodic parts interlock like fingers of folded hands, and the only interval that is ever struck simultaneously is the octave. These features have been studied extensively in *kiganda* xylophone music, which is especially rewarding because it also demonstrates practices such as octave transposition and the existence of a highly elaborate modal system guiding melodic exposition. Among others, see the following works for indepth analyses that pertain: Peter Cooke and Sam Kasule (1999); Peter Cooke (2000); Catherine Gray (1995); Gerhard Kubik (1968, 1992); Lois Anderson (1968); James Micklem, Andrew Cooke, and Mark Stone (1999).

There are several interlocking features of *kiganda* music that are specific to the *kiganda* xylophone associated with the royal Baganda court. Three musicians typically perform on a single *amadinda* and follow strict compositional rules dictated by the *role* that *each* player assumes:

- First, an *amadinda* player assumes the role of the *"omunazi,"* that is "the starter," literally the one who "throws" the main tune.
- A second player on the *amadinda* assumes the role of the *"omwawuzi,"* playing a secondary melody that "mixes" in with the first melody.

- A third role is adopted by the *"omukonezi"* amadinda player who provides a supportive, elaborating part that highlights the most important tonal features of the particular modal system used in a performance.

There are three different types of xylophone playing styles in the central Buganda kingdom that are associated with three different instruments:

Akadinda—a xylophone that typically has at least 17 keys (upwards of 22 keys)

Amadinda—a xylophone that usually has 12 keys

Akadinda ka ssekinoomu—a solo instrument, typically only played by one person, usually a xylophone with 9 keys

ACTIVITY 5.1 *The three roles on the amadinda are illustrated by three Ugandan musicians on CD track 28:*

Omunazi	begins the selection and continues through the entire selection
Omwawuzi	enters at 0:35 and continues through the entire selection
Omukonezi	enters at 1:07 and continues through the entire selection

As you listen, identify the entrances of each of the three amadinda players. Articulate the differences in their performing roles.

On CD Track 29, the Blair String Quartet demonstrates an adaptation of very similar interlocking parts as they explore parallel interdependent melodic relationships in the first movement of Tamusuza's quartet. The similarity in the *texture* of interlocking parts between CD track 28 and CD track 29 should be apparent. For a complete recording of this movement from Tamusuza's quartet see the Kronos Quartet's *Pieces of Africa* listed in the Resources section.

In this case study specific *kiganda* roots of Tamusuza's string quartet, "Mu Kkubo Ery 'Omusaalaba," were identified and outlined. Identifying such details enhances not only our appreciation for this significant and rewarding piece, but also increases our understanding of the negotiation of identity many contemporary musics engage in their interactions with modernity, calling into question any attempt to label modernity in Africa as "repudiating" traditional Baganda culture.

CASE STUDY #2: "THE ROOTS OF *BENGA*"

This second case study explores ways in which *traditional* performance and *traditional* culture intersect within the commercialization of popular culture in East Africa, specifically in Kenya. Highlighted in this case study are three musicians, traditional praise-singer and *nyatiti* [harp-lyre] player, Andericus Apondi, the "king" of *benga*, D. O. Misiani, and the young musician Lawrence Oyuga, all from the area of Kisumu, a Western port on Lake Victoria and Kenya's second largest town (see the map of East Africa, Figure 1.1). A principle goal in presenting this case study is to illustrate a specific way in which the roots of popular musical genres in East Africa can be understood as both interactive with and manipulative of modernity. A basic assumption of this case study is that traditional musics—or other closely related musical forms—often provide the source materials from which many current and historical popular genres in urban environments draw much of their creativity. *Benga* provides a clear example for considering how this assumption plays out in a contemporary context.

Benga is a style of popular music that emerged primarily from traditional string instrument playing styles, such as the style associated with the *nyatiti* lyre of the Luo people of the lakes region of Western Kenya. Until the 1970s Kenyan popular music was mostly dominated by Central African dance bands, until giving way to a new style that would become a defining national musical voice for Kenya. Musicians of the Kikuyu and Kamba peoples also participated in the development of *benga* music, contributing unique derivatives of *benga* rooted in specific ethnicities. The reflections now offered on the position of *benga* within multiple music communities are based on the author's field research in western Kenya and on the contributions of other scholars (see the *Resources* section for the works of Jean Kidula and Douglas Patterson who examine the roles of the popular music industry in Kenya. See Patterson's work in particular for further discussions of musical style in *benga*.)

The eighty-year-old traditional *nyatiti* [lyre] player, Andericus Apondi, lives today in a remote village outside of Kisumu, Kenya. Apondi has played the *nyatiti* since he was a youth and continues to this day to make a living as a musician, singing the praises of his patrons at weddings, funerals, and other celebrations. His praise-song musical style is firmly rooted in the ethnic tradition of the Luo people of

FIGURE 5.7   *Photograph of the* nyatiti.   *(Photo by Jonathan Rogers.)*

Western Kenya. CD track 31 includes a recording of a praise song in which Apondi weaves together aspects of his own life with the lives of those he is praising as he accompanies himself on the *nyatiti.*

The typical *nyatiti* performance tradition involves a solo male performer who sings while accompanying himself on the *nyatiti* (see Figure 5.7) and providing rhythmic accompaniment with *gara* (metal leg rattles) and a metal toe ring. Performances involving a *nyatiti* player may either be purely for entertainment or involve specific, predetermined reasons for praise singing. The instrument is typically featured in marriage, funeral, and cleansing rituals (see Owuor 1983). In the performance of Luo threnody, performers lament the loss of life in a particular style in which text is recited freely, interspersed with elaborate melismas and other dramatic melodic gestures. Although the music of *nyatiti* players is a necessary aspect of many traditional Luo rituals, its primary function is to entertain (see Barz 2002 for more details on Luo praise singing). Included below is a brief description of the performance style taken from the author's fieldnotes.

During a break in one of my recording sessions with Mr. Apondi I asked if there was any relationship between tradi-

tional *nyatiti playing and the* benga *popular music tradition famous in Western Kenya. Apondi nodded enthusiastically, and suggested that a clear relationship between* **all** *string-playing traditions among the Luo-speaking areas of Western Kenya existed. He smiled as he picked up his* nyatiti *again (see Figure 5.8), reattached his percussive toe ring and ankle bells, and began playing in a style that he claimed gave rise to the birth of* benga *in the 1960s.*

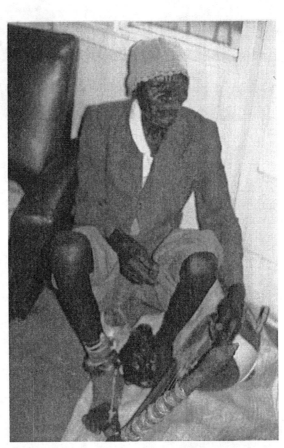

FIGURE 5.8 *Photograph of Andericus Apondi,* nyatiti *player.* (Photo by Gregory Barz.)

The demonstration of traditional Luo *nyatiti* playing in CD track 31 raises three issues clearly:

- First, the interdependence of the bass and the treble lines, the lower and higher pitched melodies, in Andericus Apondi's *nyatiti* playing are mirrored in the playful and omnipresent interaction of bass and lead guitars in *benga*, as will be demonstrated in CD track 32.

- Second, Apondi's *gara* leg rattles and his toe ring also point to the roots of what typically comprises *benga* drum patterns.

- Third, Apondi's ongoing, contemporary playing demonstrates that the Luo style of *nyatiti* praise singing that gave rise to *benga* did not fade once *benga* became popular.

Nyatiti-accompanied praise singing among the Luo should be understood as more than an older, traditional form of music making that merely contributed to the formation and development of a popular form of music in Kenya. Rather, we must keep in mind that such *nyatiti* praise singing continues today in Luo villages, and it is still an vibrant and important aspect of the everyday soundscape for many Luo performance contexts.

D. O. MISIANI, THE "KING" OF *BENGA*

Excerpt from Fieldnotes It is early evening in Kisumu, and as the sun sets over Lake Victoria the temperature seems to fall a degree every minute. Victor Mdenyo, a Kenyan traditional dancer arrives at my hotel on the shores of Lake Victoria to accompany me to a local social club to hear D. O. Misiani and his band, Shirati Jazz, play. We set out on foot, and it starts to rain as we wind our way through the town's side streets. I find it increasingly difficult to negotiate my way in the dark through the potholes now filled with muddy water.

We weave our way through the town's main bus depot passing kiosks selling sodas, toiletries, and cassettes in an area known for its social clubs and bars. I notice immediately that the power is off in the area surrounding the Crescent Inn, our destination. Without hesitating we enter the bar in complete darkness and walk to an area in back that is packed

*tightly with tables placed directly across from a roped-off area
intended for the band. Most tables are occupied with people
slowly drinking beers or bottles of Coke or Fanta in the dark.
A waitress comes over to us, putting a candle on our table
and I order two Kenyan Tusker beers for Victor and myself.
We decide to wait out the power outage to see if Misiani's
band will eventually play. "No electricity, no* benga," *Victor says to me in KiSwahili.*

*As the rain pours down harder on the bar's tin roof I hear
an attempt to start a generator outside the club. After a few
minutes Victor nudges me, and points to an old man in a
white shirt with an electric guitar slung across his chest sitting in a dark corner across the room. It is obviously Misiani,
the much heralded "king of* benga." *I catch my breath as I
watch him stroke the strings of his guitar, as if playing a song
silently to himself. The generator finally kicks in power just
as the main electricity is restored to the building, and the
speakers begin to blast recorded contemporary* benga *tunes at
an incredibly high volume. I shout across the table to Victor,
asking him if he knows how old Misiani is. He considers the
question for a minute and then responds that he thinks he
must be very, very old, perhaps forty. I chuckle since my own
observation puts Misiani's age at sixty. I am momentarily
distracted by the live* benga *ensemble, comprising four electric and bass guitars, plugging their guitars into the same amp.*

*As the other band members begin to make their way over
to the roped-off area it becomes clear that there are more backup
singers than there are instrumentalists. Many people appear
to have some connection to the band—singers, dancers, and
instrumentalists. The guitarists begin a lengthy period of tuning, after which the band opens with their signature piece,
"Joshirati Misiani," which translates to "Misiani and Shirati Jazz," a song of self-praise in which the group congrat-
ulates itself for being so good, for being No. 1., for being the
kings and queens of Kisumu-style* benga. *Many people get
up to dance immediately, carrying their beers and cigarettes
with them, and I begin to feel awkward for remaining solidly
rooted in my chair. The band finishes their first extended*

song, and I am the only one who claps. No one else joins in. As the band continues, I notice that none of the musicians look at each other directly as they play. No one in the social club appears to pay any attention to the musicians, and I begin to suspect that such interaction must be discouraged. But, this is the king of benga! *I try to readjust my listening to become more passive, more detached, to appear less interested, but I keep returning to the rock solid guitar licks and the close interaction between the bass and supporting guitars.*

Daniel Owino ("D. O.") Misiani along with his group Shirati Jazz became the first great interpreters of the emerging *benga* style in the 1960s. Other innovators of the Luo *benga* tradition include the Victoria Kings (named for their location near Lake Victoria) and George Ramogi. Misiani continues to perform several evenings each week at the Crescent Inn in the town of Kisumu, considered by many to be the birthplace of *benga*. (*Note:* for further reading on *benga* and on D. O. Misiani see Stapleton and May 1990.)

The early efforts of D. O. Misiani, George Ramogi, and others to incorporate elements of Luo traditional music in *benga* and other popular music genres continue today. Lawrence Oyuga leads a local Kisumu-based band known as the Kabila Klan [*"kabila"* is a KiSwahili term for "ethnic group" or "clan," and coupled with "Klan" creates an interesting double emphasis on "ethnicity" or traditional culture in the group's name]. The group represents the best of the upcoming generation of popular musicians working in western Kenya. In CD track 31, a recording of Kabila Klan performing "Jo Piny" ["The People of the World"]. sung in the Luo language, composer and arranger Lawrence Oyuga suggests that everyone needs to change their lifestyles and behavior in response to many societal concerns in the area. The adaptation of the *nyatiti* performance style by the Kabila Klan guitarists is clearly audible in this example as they imitate the distinct musical roles typically assumed by the *nyatiti*. "Jo Piny" features repetitive lyrics supported by an interactive harmony supplied by the guitars, a defining critical feature of *benga*. The characteristics of *benga* guitar style playing are a fast beat and a prominent, "in-your-face" bass guitar line. The bass guitar typically established the *benga* groove by inserting brief melodic riffs that frequently start and stop. The electric guitars typically enter at the end of each vocal phrase with their individual, catchy riffs. The bass and lead guitars also weave melodic patterns together, asserting strong individual yet interdependent roles. Members of Kabila Klan performing on CD track 31 include: Kevin Ian Omondi (drums and voice), Steve Simba (lead guitar), Tom Jack Nyanga (rattles), Peter Okongo (guitar), and Lawrence M. Oyuga (bass guitar and voice). This track was recorded by Steven Samba in Kisumu.

"Jo Piny"	"The People of the World"
Kabili wa wacho ma kendo	Ethnic groups, we tell you we are
wabiro gi manyien,	coming with a new one,
Hero kanyo kanyo	Just there, there
En ang'oma timo jo piny?	What is happing to the people
	of world?
Baba lok pach be lam	Dad, change your mind and pray
Mama lok pach be lam	Mom, change your mind and pray
Dungu lok pach be lam	Brother change your mind and pray
Dada lok pach be lam	Sister change your mind and pray
Dana lok pach be lam	Grandmother, change your mind
	and pray
Be lam	Come pray

CONCLUSION: POPULAR VERSUS TRADITIONAL—"MODERNITY HAPPENED!"

Why focus on the musical and cultural boundaries specific to *benga* in East Africa? Why spend the time and effort to locate the boundaries in any popular music in East Africa (and by extension other regions of sub-Saharan Africa)? Locating boundaries, as the scenario above suggests, must include the traditional Luo roots of *benga* within *nyatiti* praise singing and thus help us situate and understand popular expressive culture (music, art, dance, and drama) within greatly enlarged cultural and historical contexts. Responses to modernity—as in the twentieth-century changes that have occurred in African expressive culture—are partially in response to increased participation in systems of international trade and commerce. According to ethnomusicologist Gerhard Kubik, significant changes within African musics have occurred in large part due to the ongoing development of two particular socioeconomic issues:

> *First,* the physical opening up of sub-Saharan Africa created opportunities for people to travel via new forms of transportation (i.e.,

steamers, motor vehicles, and later air travel). Areas that historically had little contact with each other, except via the eighteenth- and nineteenth-century caravan trade routes, suddenly became neighbors. This opening up of the continent created cultural dislocation, facilitating the emergence of urban, industrial, and mining centers, and thereby promoting labor migration, inter-ethnic and inter-language contact, and agglomerations of townships. *Second*, the rise of mass media, marked by the availability of wireless sets and hand-cranked gramophones from the 1920s onwards, meant that songs could spread to remote villages without human carriers. In the late nineteenth century, musical instruments such as the *zeze* (flat-bar zither) had reached Kisangani on the Congo river with porters traveling from Bagamoyo (Tanzania) along a caravan trade route. But by the 1940s, new songs began to spread by radio signals and shellac discs through the Belgian Congo, and original performers were rarely seen. ("Africa," *New Grove Dictionary of Music and Musicians*, 2000)

Benga followed specific and similar patterns of geographic migratory patterns and social networks, eventually reaching beyond Kenyan listeners, beyond the geographic boundaries of East Africa. But just as *benga* was finally reaching international markets in the 1980s, newer forms of Central (not East) African dance musics—*soukous, kwassa kwassa,* and *rumba* among others—began to assume an increasing prominence and market share in the globalization of the African popular music industry.

The shift away from *benga* in the global consciousness is typical of the directions "popular" music has taken as exportable (and expendable) African commodities. Thus, as a concept applied to African expressive culture, "popular music" is perhaps an artificial construction. Maintaining a distinction between traditional and modern music has only recently (and sometimes reluctantly) been accepted in sub-Saharan Africa, and in many ways such a distinction is a biased division. Such a division is not without precedent, however. During the 1970s in Tanzania, for example, government officials began to rely on this distinction, replicating the traditional-modern dichotomy—*muziki ya asili* (or *muziki ya kienyeji*) versus *musiki ya Ulaya* (traditional music versus music of Europe)—for political means.

Many different styles of African musics that non-African listeners might casually refer to as "traditional" from an outsiders' perspective are in fact very popular in that they are listened to and consumed in specific ways by many people. It is often incorrect, therefore, to speak of "traditional" music merely because locally produced acoustic or non-electric musical instrument—such as xylophones, lamellophones, and drums—are used within a performance. Similarly, it might just be as equally incorrect to speak of "popular" music merely because electric guitars, electronic keyboards, or synthesizers dominate the expressive resources of a musical example.

Presenting any particular African popular music as a tradition with strong, enforced boundaries—whether by insiders or outsiders—is problematic, as the example of *benga* included in this chapter illustrates. *Benga* participates in and evokes multiple worlds—traditional, popular, elite, and religious—for its varied performers and for its varied audiences. Distinctions are often troublesome to musicians themselves, especially in this region of the world. Careful attention therefore must be paid to the application of foreign terminology to emergent, developing, and historical music cultures of East Africa, and if at all possible we might consider refraining from the uncritical use of categorizations worked out in other parts of the world in relation to African cultural areas that are in many ways different aesthetically and culturally.

As a possible means for addressing the presumed popular-versus-traditional dichotomy ethnomusicologist Gerhard Kubik suggests that we consider adapting the term "musical traditions." In a sense, musical traditions can refer to expressive musical forms that are passed along from one generation to the next during a finite period of time, irrespective of stylistic considerations, presence or absence of presumed foreign influences, degree of so-called popularity, or the kind of instruments that are used. A musical tradition can apply to any musical form regardless of its popularity or status within traditional culture. It is legitimate, as Kubik suggests, to speak of the Katanga guitar style, for example, which began in the mid-1940s along the Copperbelt of the Central African Katanga Province (extending from Angola through the Democratic Republic of Congo to Zambia), as a specific musical tradition because there have been second- and third-generation guitarists expressing themselves in that style since the 1940s. Thus, if the Katanga guitar style was reduced to "popular music" we might very well obscure important and essentially historical questions. The Katanga guitar style was extremely popular in the 1950s and early 1960s (as witnessed by the guitarist Mwenda Jean Bosco's famous travels to East Africa—Nairobi and Dar es Salaam—and his advertisements for *Dawa ya Kweli* on the radio in that region), yet this style would later be superseded by the western Congolese electric guitar styles of Kasanda wa Mikalay ("Dr. Nico"), Luambo "Franco" Makiadi, and others who defined with their prolific recordings and performances the dominant styles of lead guitar playing for the Democratic Republic of Congo in the 1970s and 1980s.

This might lead us to suggest that there is really no such thing as popular music as a category in East Africa; any musical genre depending on specific historically active forces can rise to popularity under favorable circumstances. For example, as detailed in this chapter, *benga* in East Africa was an outgrowth of a specific string-band tradition that rose to the status of popular music not only in urban areas but also regionally throughout East Africa from the 1960s until the present time.

CHAPTER 6

Cooling Down!

INTRODUCTION

Traditional musical performance was presented in the first chapter of this volume as an organic whole, what Ruth Stone refers to elsewhere as a "constellation of the arts" (Stone 2000, 7). This is indeed the way many traditional musics have been presented to this author by his field colleagues and fellow musicians in East Africa. Centurio Balikoowa, for example, defended this organicism to the author once when asked to separate different aspects of a particular dance for recording purposes:

> That is why I sang when I played the *endingidi* for you. You find that in our traditional music you play the music, you sing, and you dance. If you are dancing you might also find yourself playing an instrument and you sing. In our music, we say that the instruments *accompany* the dancing. You play an instrument to accompany the dancers. You sing to accompany the instruments. And, you dance to accompany the singing.

TRADITIONAL MUSIC AND THE INTERRELATION OF THE ARTS IN EAST AFRICA

Traditional music represents unity for Balikoowa and for other musicians in this area of the world, and as such represents an *interdependent interrelation of the arts* in East Africa.

> Excerpt from Fieldnotes. *It is Sunday morning at the Power of Jesus Around the World Church located along the outskirts of Kisumu, Kenya. I sit on one of many crowded benches as do the several hundred others attending an open-air church prayer meeting. The steamy temperature has risen considerably despite the early hour. The congregation is in-*

vited to begin the service by laying their hands on a group of
individuals who recently lost a male family member. Before
long, one of the service's leaders begins to speak in tongues.
The bereaved members all fall to the ground as they too begin proclaiming in what are to me unintelligible statements.
Within minutes a large portion of the congregation is swept
up in the spirit and the emotion of the moment and they too
begin to speak in tongues as many wave their hands high in
the air in gestures of praise and thanksgiving. The grieving
members of the congregation are cared for and consoled by
church leaders and elders, and after an extended period of
time one of the pastors begins the call of a well-known chorus, singing into a generator-powered microphone. The give
and take between the soloist and the congregation builds up
gradually, and the congregation soon fully participates in the
chorus known in many parts of North America as "Kumbaya" (CD track 32).

The spirit healing session *cools down* after a half hour or so, and the performance of "Kumbaya" presented on CD track 32 reunites the community, giving them back "language" while at the same time bringing
the church congregation back to their seats. The Caribbean and North
American roots of this simple chorus, while not forefronted in the minds
of many participants, is nevertheless present; this performance of "Kumbaya" is sung in English, causing an interruption in the Luo and
KiSwahili languages that had up until this point dominated the wor-
ship service.

This volume now closes with the same voices that were used to open
this study of traditional music in East Africa. Lawrence Chiteri, a teacher
and leader of the dance troupe, the New Horizon Players in Kisumu,
Kenya (Figure 1.1) and Ayisha Kyamugisha, a dancer and trainer with
the Ndere Troupe in Kampala, Uganda (Figure 1.2), reflect on the cultural connection made by and for performance of traditional music and
dance. Chiteri responds to a query concerning what he would want people to know about East African music in general, or Kenyan music
specifically:

Well, Kenyans cling to different social and cultural tenets, which they
continue to express in their songs. *Ngoma, and I use that term to refer
to all traditional songs and dances, are basically a means of communicating*

what our culture is all about, what we believe in our society, what our customs are all about, in an indigenous way. So, naturally, our indigenous Kenyan music must differ from Ugandan music, even though we are both East Africans, there are distinct ethnic affiliations to which we ascribe and to which we are exposed in our everyday lives. Singing and dancing are a very important part of this. So, for example, if you focus on the Luo people, the way they dance and perform traditional music will only exhibit what the Luo believe, and this will not be the same as what people in Buganda, in Uganda, exhibit. Even within a twenty-minute drive outside this province in Kenya, you will find the Luyia singing and dancing traditional music, which express only what *they* do, which is not similar to what people do here. *So, the cultural curtain also decides which types of ngoma are performed.* Among my people, the Luyia, we sing circumcision songs, initiation songs, even beer-drinking songs which are performed quite differently from those of the Luo people. They might even have a different version of one of our *ngoma* to celebrate the same ceremony, communicate the same mood, and enact the same initiation that we have . . . even among the Maasai, the songs they sing do not correspond with the songs people of the Western Province sing. So, somehow there must be a difference, and that difference is very striking. It just requires a little bit of time to recognize, but if there is difference twenty miles down the road, why would we not expect the same type of differences within the United States? It's very wonderful and very curious at the same time, isn't it?

Today, traditional musical performances (Chiteri uses the term *"ngoma"* several times) exist in multiple worlds in East Africa, yet remain firmly rooted behind traditional and meaningful "cultural curtains," often a mere "twenty miles down the road." In the aforementioned excerpt from a field interview, Chiteri confirms several of the main tenets of traditional music set out in this volume.

• *Traditional Music Performances* communicate within and contribute to the formation of both culture and community.

• *Traditional Music Performances* communicate at local, national, and global levels not only what it means to be a member of a particular community (or "tribe" or ethnic group), but also what it means to be Kenyan, to be Tanzanian, to be Uganda, as well as what it means to be African.

• *Traditional Music Performances* communicate many of the most important roles and functions of local and regional customs by asserting indigenous ideals of voluntary associations and social indemnity (community support) groups.

- *Traditional Music Performances* bring individuals together and hold them together, uniting them by communicating and affirming communally held morals and values.

One of the most critical responses to the issues of modernity discussed in Chapter 5 can be clearly demonstrated in the shift of style used to perform traditional music by national and cultural dance troupes in urban centers such as Dar es Salaam (Tanzania), Kisumu and Nairobi (Kenya), and Kampala (Uganda). While the "bits" that contribute to an overall understanding of an individual dance may be changed or adapted to a particular performance venue in urban contexts, the core or central stylistic features of a dance must often remain the same for traditional music to be understood as an indigenous or local musical expression. In the following excerpt from a field interview, Ayisha Kyamugisha provides several details concerning aspects of change and adaptation that exist today between rural and urban contexts as she responds to the query about whether there is a difference between performing music dances with the Ndere Troupe in the city of Kampala compared to performing in a village, a difference between the ways traditional Ugandan village music is represented to urban audiences compared to its roots, its traditional contexts?

AYISHA: Somehow it is different, yes, because in our villages we do not *perform* village music in the same way as we do here in the cities. We are not exposed to very large audiences in villages. There we are not expected to adjust constantly to new performance venues. *The way we used to dance in the olden days, well, that is how we still dance it in the villages. It has not developed in that sense.* But, in the cities, professional troupes such as the Ndere Troupe have had to adapt to performing for large and diverse audiences. We now dance in very particular ways for particular audiences. But, again, in the villages they dance the way they've always danced.

AUTHOR: Will *Baakisimba* always be performed the same way with Ndere or do they change or vary over time?

AYISHA: Somehow *Baakisimba*, for example, has already changed a bit. But the defining characteristics, the movement from the waist, will always remain the same. For us we put different *designs* into our choreography, but the typical features remain the same.

AUTHOR: So, if *you* were to perform a *kisoga* dance in Busoga, would it be any different than if you were to perform it in Buganda, for example at the Nile Hotel in Kampala?

AYISHA: OK, there might be a difference because of the expectations of the older people in the villages. For us we learn *on the spot* whenever we perform for them. We are not as flexible as the original people are. There are things that they can do which we cannot because of our training in so many different traditions. *We are not totally inside any one tradition.* So, ultimately I guess we do in fact perform traditional musics differently. It's not the way that those people used to dance that people now are dancing. It keeps on changing. *We modernize it according to the experiences that we acquire.*

With Chiteri's and Ayisha's sentiments this volume has now *cooled down,* and this conclusion brings the outward-reaching focus of the previous chapters back to a more specific statement of the power of traditional music making in historic and contemporary East Africa, and the

FIGURE 6.1 *A performance by the Atuwa Troupe of a newly composed* ngoma, Baalero, *performed in Bugoba Village, Uganda.* (Photo by Gregory Barz.)

ability of traditional music to communicate *who one is* in direct relationship to *who one is not*. As demonstrated throughout this text, the performance of traditional music is typically used to mark significant moments in the life cycle, to punctuate communal rituals, to underscore social behavior, and to facilitate political and economic education. Throughout this volume ways in which traditional performances are used to mediate conflict or disastrous situations, such as seasons of drought, were introduced. In many communities music also assumes or is assigned a didactic role, such as when musicians and community leaders are empowered to use music to educate about impending problems and concerns, such as famine and family planning.

Traditional music remains a significant marker of identity in many aspects of East African communities and societies; it is central, as Chiteri suggests previously, to the construction of historical constructions of self and other in the region as well as to the performance of everyday religious and spiritual life (see Figure 6.1 for a performance of newly composed performance of traditional music, *Baalero*, performed in Bugoba Village, Uganda). Traditional music and dance in Kenya, Uganda, and Tanzania today constantly shifts between two (perhaps more!) worlds, often retaining roots in village traditions while embracing change, adaptation, and modernity in wonderfully unique, wonderfully East African ways.

Glossary

What follows is a select glossary of the most important terms introduced in this volume. Each of these terms is pronounced on CD track 33.

akadinda: xylophone of the Baganda people, 17 keys (upwards of 22 keys) (Uganda)

akadinda ka ssekinoomu: xylophone of the Baganda people, typically played by one person, usually 9 keys

amadinda: xylophone of the Baganda people, usually 12 keys

Baakisimba: music dance of the Baganda people (Uganda)

Bagaalu: traditional dance society of the Sukuma people (Tanzania)

Bagiika: traditional dance society of the Sukuma people (Tanzania)

bufumu: manipulation of divinatory forces, Sukumaland (Tanzania)

Bugóbogóbo: *mbiina* of the Sukuma people (Tanzania)

Bulabo: feast of Corpus Christi, Sukumaland (Tanzania)

Chakacha: *ngoma* of the WaSwahili people of (Tanzania, Kenya)

embaire: xylophone of the Basoga people (Uganda)

endere: flute of the Baganda people (Uganda)

endingidi: tubefiddle of the Basoga people (Uganda)

filimbi: whistle of the Sukuma people (Tanzania)

filulu: small, two-hole aerophone of the Sukuma people (Tanzania)

kabaka: Bagandan king (Uganda)

kaswida: songs (KiSwahili)

khanga: a woman's cloth wrap with sayings in KiSwahili printed on them

kiganda: refers to music of the Baganda people of Uganda

mapambio: short, local songs (KiSwahili)

mbunifu: "designer" of music (KiSwahili)

msanifu: "composer" of music (KiSwahili)

mwalimu: teacher (KiSwahili)

ngoma: music/song/dance in several (but not all) parts of East Africa

ntongooli: 8-string lyre (Uganda)

nyatiti: lyre of the Luo people of Kenya

nyimbo: songs (KiSwahili)

wigaashe: "sitting song," Sukumaland (Tanzania)

Resources

Reading

An excellent place to start for a general overview of issues related to the study of music and expressive culture in sub-Saharan Africa is Gerhard Kubik's "Africa" overview article in *The New Grove Dictionary of Music and Musicians* (London 2000). Another fascinating overview of the entire continent and sections devoted to East Africa is the multiauthored volume, *The Garland Handbook of African Music*, edited by Ruth Stone (New York: Garland, 2000). For more specific musical information concerning individual countries covered in this volume see the individual country articles in *New Grove*: "Tanzania" (also by Kubik), "Uganda" (by Peter Cooke), and "Kenya" (by William Umbima). Each country article in the *New Grove* includes a detailed bibliography and discography, as well as further information supporting various traditional music forms found throughout East Africa. *The New Grove* "Ngoma" article written by East African specialist Peter Cooke also provides useful, supplementary material and historical resources.

The New Grove also includes several articles of interest on individual East African artist-musicians including Siti Bint Saad (Zanzibari *taarab* singer), Remmy Ongala (Tanzanian singer and composer), Mwenda Jean Bosco (Congolese composer famous throughout East Africa), Fundi Konde (Kenyan popular musician), Hukwe Zawose (Tanzanian traditional musician), and Gideon Mdegella (Tanzanian composer). Genres covering in *The New Grove* worth referencing include: *taarab, kwaya, benga,* and *ngoma*. Entries in the dictionary on instruments and instrumental types that pertain include: marimba, Katanga guitar style, lamellophone, xylophone, harp (Africa), drum-chime, and drum.

The general list of print resource materials provided below is intended to serve as a springboard for those interested in more specific features of music, dance, and drama not only in East Africa, but also in Africa in general. In addition, sources cited within the text of this volume are also given complete references.

Anderson, Lois. 1968. *The Miko System of Kiganda Xylophone Music*. PhD dissertation, UCLA.

Askew, Kelly M. 2000. "Following in the Tracks of *Beni*: The Diffusion of the Tanga *Taarab Tradition*." In *Mashindano! Competitive Music Performance in East Africa*, Gregory Barz and Frank Gunderson, eds. Dar es Salaam: Mkuki wa Nyota; Oxford: African Books Collective Ltd.

———. 2002. *Performing The Nation: Swahili Music and Cultural Politics in Tanzania*. Chicago: University of Chicago Press.

Barz, Gregory F. 1997. "Confronting the Field(note) In and Out of the Field: Music, Voices, Texts, and Experiences in Dialogue." In *Shadows in the Field: New Perspectives for Fieldwork in Ethnomusicology*, Gregory F. Barz and Timothy J. Cooley eds. Oxford and New York: Oxford University Press.

———. 2000a. "*Tamati*: Music Competition and Community Formation: an Epilogue," *Mashindano! Competitive Music Performance in East Africa*, Gregory Barz and Frank Gunderson, eds. Dar es Salaam: Mkuki na Nyota (Oxford: African Books Collective).

———. 2000b. "Politics of Remembering: Performing History(-ies) in Youth *Kwaya* Competitions in Dar es Salaam, Tanzania." In *Mashindano! Competitive Music Performance in East Africa*, Gregory Barz and Frank Gunderson, eds. Dar es Salaam: Mkuki na Nyota (Oxford: African Books Collective).

———. 2002. "Meaning in *Benga* Music of Western Kenya," *British Journal of Ethnomusicology* 10/8, 109–17.

———. 2003. *Performing Religion: Negotiating Past and Present in Kwaya Music of Tanzania*. Amsterdam: Editions Rodopi.

Berliner, Paul. 1978. *The Soul of Mbira*. Berkeley: University of California Press.

Bessire, Aimee and Mark Bessire. 1997. *Sukuma*. Rosen Publishing Group.

Blacking, John. 1980. "Political and Musical Freedom in the Music of Some Black South African Churches." In *The Structure of Folk Models* (ASA Monograph 20), L. Holy and M. Stuchlik, eds. London: Academic Press.

———. 1987. "Intention and Change in the Performance of European Hymns by Some Black South African Churches." In *Transplanted European Music Cultures: Miscellanea Musicologica* (Adelaide Studies in Musicology 12), G. Moon, ed. Adelaide.

Campbell, Carol A. and Carol M. Eastman. 1984. "*Ngoma*: Swahili Adult Song Performance in Context." *Ethnomusicology* 28/3. 467–93.

Chernoff, John Miller. 1979. *African Rhythm and African Sensibility: Aesthetics and Social Action in African Musical Idioms*. Chicago: University of Chicago Press.

Conant, Faith. 1988. "Adjogbo in Lom*: Music and Musical Terminology of the Ge." MA Thesis, Tufts University.

Cooke, Peter and Sam Kasule. 1999. "The Musical Scene in Uganda: Views from Without and Within." *African Music*, vii/4.

Cooke, Peter R. 2000. "Appeasing the Spirits: Music, Possession, Divination and Healing in Busoga, Eastern Uganda," *Indigenous Religious Musics*, Graham Harvey and Karen Ralls-MacLeod, eds. London: Ashgate.

Coplan, David B. 1994. *In the Time of Cannibals: The Word Music of South Africa's Basotho Migrants*. Chicago: University of Chicago Press.

Erlmann, Veit. 1991a. " 'The Past is Far and the Future is Far': Power and Performance Among Zulu Migrant Workers." Draft MS Prepared for the African Studies Workshop of the University of Chicago.

————. 1991b. *African Stars: Studies in Black South African Performance*. Chicago: University of Chicago Press.

Friedson, Steven. 1996. *Dancing Prophets: Musical Experience in Tumbuka Healing*. Chicago: University of Chicago Press.

Glassie, Henry. 1982. *Passing the Time in Ballymenone: Culture and History of an Ulster Community*. Philadelphia: University of Pennsylvania Press.

Gray, Catherine T. 1995. "Compositional Techniques in Roman Catholic Church Music in Uganda." *British Journal of Ethnomusicology*, iv, 135–55.

Gunderson, Frank. 1999. *Music Labor Associations in Sukumaland, Tanzania: History and Practice*. PhD dissertation, Wesleyan University.

————. 2000a. "Witchcraft, Witcraft, and Musical Warfare: The Rise of the *Bagiika-Bagaalu* Music Competitions in Sukumaland, Tanzania." In *Mashindano! Competitive Music Performance in East Africa*, Gregory Barz and Frank Gunderson, eds. Dar es Salaam: Mkuki na Nyota (Oxford: African Books Collective).

————. 2000b. " '*Kifungua Kinywa*,' or Opening the Contest with Chai." In *Mashindano! Competitive Music Performance in East Africa*, Gregory Barz and Frank Gunderson, eds. Dar es Salaam: Mkuki na Nyota (Oxford: African Books Collective).

Hopton-Jones, Pamela. 1995. "Introducing the Music of East Africa." *Music Educators Journal* 82/3, 26–30.

Janzen, John. 1992. *Ngoma: Discourse of Healing in Central and Southern Africa*. Berkeley: University of California Press.

Kidula, Jean Ngoya. 1998. '*Sing and Shine': Religious Popular Music in Kenya (Television, Gospel Music)*. PhD dissertation, University of California, Los Angeles.

Kisliuk, Michelle. 1993. "Confronting the Quintessential: Singing, Dancing, and Everyday Life Among Biaka Pygmies (Central African Republic)." PhD dissertation. New York University.

————. 1997. *Seize the Dance! BaAka Musical Life and the Ethnography of Performance*. New York: Oxford University Press.

Kubik, Gerhard. 1968. "Court Music in Uganda: Recordings of Xylophone Compositions Preserved in the Phonogrammarchiv of the Austrian

Academy of Sciences, Vienna." *International Committee on Urgent Anthropological and Ethnological Research Bulletin*, x, 41–51.

———. 1992. "Embaire Xylophone Music of Samusiri Babalanda (Uganda 1968)." *World of Music: Journal of the International Institute for Traditional Music*, xxxiv/1, 57–84.

———. 2000. "Africa: Twentieth-century Features." *New Grove Dictionary of Music and Musicians*. London: Macmillan.

Locke, David. 1979. "The Music of Atsiagbeko." PhD dissertation, Wesleyan University.

Makubuya, James. 1995. " 'Endongo': The Role and Significance of the Baganda Bowl Lyre of Uganda." PhD dissertation, UCLA.

Mbele, Joseph L. 2000. "Gindu Nkima: A Sukuma Heroine" In *Mashindano! Competitive Music Performance in East Africa*, Gregory Barz and Frank Gunderson, eds. Dar es Salaam: Mkuki na Nyota (Oxford: African Books Collective).

Merriam, Alan P. 1964. *The Anthropology of Music*. Evanston: Northwestern University Press.

Micklem, James, Andrew Cooke, and Mark Stone. 1999. "Xylophone Music of Uganda: The Embaire of Nakibembe, Busoga." *African Music*, vii/4.

Mitchell, Frank. 1978. *Navajo Blessingway Sing: The Autobiography of Frank Mitchell, 1881–1967*, Charlotte J. Frisbie and David McAllester, eds. Tucson: University of Arizona Press.

Muller, Carol. 1999. *Rituals of Fertility and the Sacrifice of Desire: Nazarite Women's Performance in South Africa*. Chicago: University of Chicago Press.

Nannyonga-Tamusuza, Sylvia. 2003. "Competitions in School Festivals: A Process of Re-Inventing *Baakisimba* Music and Dance of the Baganda (Uganda)." *The World of Music*, xlv/1, 97–118.

Nettl, Bruno. 1983. *The Study of Ethnomusicology: Twenty-nine Issues and Concepts*. Urbana: University of Illinois Press.

Nketia, J.H. Kwabena. 1974. *The Music of Africa*. New York: W.W. Norton & Company.

Patterson, Douglas. 1986/7. "Kenya: The Business of Pleasure, part I/II." *Africa Beat* 5/6.

———. 2000. "Kenya: Life and Times of Kenyan Pop." In *World Music: The Rough Guide*. London: Rough Guides, 509–22.

Serwadda, W. Moses. 1974. *Songs and Stories from Uganda*. Danbury, CT: World Music Press.

Shelemay, Kay Kaufman. 1991. *A Song of Longing: An Ethiopian Journey*. Urbana: University of Illinois Press.

Songoyi, Elias. 1997. "The Artist and the State in Tanzania: A Study of Two Singers: Kalikali and Mwinamila." MA thesis, University of Dar es Salaam.

Stapleton, Chris and Chris May. 1990. *African Rock: The Pop Music of a Continent*. New York: Dutton.

Stone, Ruth. 2000. "African Music in a Constellation of Arts." *The Garland Handbook of African Music*. New York: Garland, 7–12.

Stewart, Gary. 1992. *Breakout: Profiles in African Rhythm*. Chicago: University of Chicago Press.

Sullivan, Lawrence E, ed. 1997. *Enchanting Powers: Music in the World's Religions*. Cambridge, MA: Harvard University Press.

Titon, Jeff Todd. 1977. *Early Downhome Blues: A Musical and Cultural Analysis*. Urbana: University of Illinois Press.

———. 1988. *Powerhouse for God: Speech, Chant, and Song in an Appalachian Baptist Church*. Austin: University of Texas Press.

Topp Fargion, Janet. 1993. "The Role of Women in Taarab in Zanzibar: An Historical Examination of a Process of 'Africanisation.'" *World of Music* 35/2.

———. 2000. "Hot Kabisa! The Mpasho Phenomenon and Taarab in Zanzibar." In *Mashindano! Competitive Music Performance in East Africa*, Gregory Barz and Frank Gunderson, eds. Dar es Salaam: Mkuki wa Nyota (Oxford: African Books Collective Ltd.).

van Dijk, Rijk. 2000. *The Quest for Fruition through Ngoma: The Political Aspects of Healing in Southern Africa*. Athens, OH: Ohio University Press.

Wachsmann, K. P. 1953. "The Sounding Instruments." In *Tribal Crafts of Uganda*, Margaret Trowell. Oxford: Oxford University Press, 309–407 and continuing plates.

Waterman, Christopher Alan. 1990. *Jùjú: A Social History and Ethnography of an African Popular Music*. Chicago: University of Chicago Press.

Listening

The lists provided below are intended to reference only recorded sound materials that are readily available for purchase or consultation in many school, college, or university libraries. Other historically important archival and out-of-print recordings are available for consultation in specialized collections, but these are not included in this resource guide. The lists below are organized according to country, yet several recordings include materials that cross individual country borders. Included within the Kenya listing is a specialized sublist of available recordings that supplements the section on *benga*.

East Africa—General
East Africa: Ceremonial and Folk Music. New York: Nonesuch Explorer Series H 72063, 2002. Compact disc. Field recordings originally from Uganda, Kenya, and Tanzania in 1975, rereleased with notes by David Fanshawe.

East Africa: Witchcraft and Ritual Music. New York: Elektra Nonesuch H-72066, 2002. Compact disc. Field recordings from Kenya and Tanzania, originally from 1975, rereleased with notes by David Fanshawe.

Kenya

Folk Music of Kenya. Nairobi: Music Therapy International, 2000. Compact disc. Music for mixed chorus and percussion, featuring the Music Therapy International Choir, directed by David Akombo.

Kenya Dance Mania. Earthworks/Virgin Records, Inc. 3-1024-2, 1991. Compact disc. Rumba and *benga* music performed by various artists in Swahili, Luo, English, Taita and Kikuyu.

Luo Roots: Musical Currents from Western Kenya, GlobeStyle CDORBD 061, 1990. Compact disc. Performances featuring Kapere Jazz, Ogwang Lelo Okoth, and Orchestra Nyanza Success.

Missa Luba: An African Mass; Kenyan Folk Melodies. Guido Haazen, comp., Boniface Mganga, cond. Philips 426 836-2, 1990. Compact disc. Muungano National Choir of Kenya performing a famous setting of the Roman Catholic mass in "Congolese" style along with Kenyan folk melodies.

Music of East Africa: Ethnic Music Classics, 1925–48, The Secret Museum of Mankind, Yazoo 7015, 1998. Compact disc. Music from East Africa compiled from 78 rpm recordings, remastered directly from original 78s.

Music of the Waswahili of Lamu, Kenya, 3 vols. Washington: Smithsonian Folkways Records FE 4093–5, 1999. 3 compact discs. Islamic music and secular traditional dance music sung in Swahili. Field recordings by Alan Boyd in Lamu, Kenya, 1976–77.

Musiques du Nyanza, Ocora, Harmonia Mundi C560022/23, 1993. Compact disc. Folk songs, chants and dances of the Luo, Gusii, and Kuria people of Nyanza (modern-day Kenya)

Roots! African Drums. Denon DC-8559, 1993. Compact disc. National Percussion Group of Kenya performing traditional dance songs and music of Kenya.

The Rough Guide to the Music of Kenya and Tanzania. London: World Music Network RGNET 1007, 1996. Compact disc. Popular and traditional music of Kenya and Tanzania accompanies the *Rough Guide to Kenya* travel guide.

The Swahili Song Book. Todtnauberg: Dizim Records 4502-2, 1999. Compact disc. Performances by Zein l'Abdin ('ud, vocals), Omari Saleh (dumbak), and Ahmed Alamoody (rika).

Benga *and Roots of* Benga
The Nairobi Beat: Kenyan Pop Music Today, Rounder 5030

Before Benga Vol. 1: Kenya Dry, Original Music OMCD 021
Before Benga Vol. 2: The Nairobi Sound, Original Music OMCD 022
Sam Chege's Ultra-Benga: *Kickin' Kikuyu-Style*, Original Music OMCD 039
Kapere Jazz Band & Others: *Luo Roots: Musical Currents from Western Kenya*, Globestyle CDORB 061
D. O. Misiani & Shirati Band: *Benga Blast!*, Earthworks STEW13CD
D. O. Misiani & Shirati Band: *Piny Ose Mer/The World Upside Down*, GlobeStyle CDORB 046
D. O. Misiani & Shirati Band: *Benga Beat*, World Circuit WCB003 (LP only)
Ayub Ogada: *En Mana Kuoyo*, Real World [CAROL 2335-2 in USA]
George Ramogi and C.K. Dumbe Dumbe Jazz Band: *1994 USA Tour—Safari ya Ligingo*, Dumbe Dumbe Records, Dumbe 01
Victoria Kings: *The Mighty Kings of Benga*, GlobeStyle CDORB 079

Tanzania
Chibite. Hukwe Ubi Zawose. Caroline Records CAR 2358-2, 1996. Compact disc. Traditional compositions by Hukwe Zawose. Performers: Hukwe Ubi Zawose, vocals and *ilimba* (lamellophone), *izeze* (traditional chordophone), *filimbi* (traditional aerophone), *nguga* (ankle bells); Charles Zawose, vocal, *ilimbas*.
Dada Kidawa [Sister Kidawa]. Original Music OMCD032, 1995. Compact disc. Popular dance band music from Tanzania featuring the Cuban Marimba Band, Kiko Kids Jazz, Kilwa Jazz Band, Western Jazz Band, NUTA Jazz Band, National Jazz Band, Atomic Jazz Band, Dar es Salaam Jazz Band, and Njohole Jazz Band. Recorded during the 1960s.
Guitar Songs from Tanzania, Zambia, and Zaire. Original OMCD023, 1990. Compact disc. Acoustic-guitar recordings from the 1950s and '60s. Recorded by John Low.
Maisha: musiques de Tanzanie, Musique du monde, Buda 92546-2, 1995. Compact disc. Traditional music of the Makonde people of Tanzania.
Mambo. Remmy Ongala. Real World 92129-2, 1992. Compact disc. Tanzanian popular musician Remmy (Ramzani Mtoro) Ongala with his band Orchestra Super Matimila.
Masumbi: musique de divertissement wagogo [Wagogo entertainment music]. Ocora, Harmonia Mundi C 560165, 2002. Compact disc. Field recordings by Philippe Malidin. in the villages of Nzali, Majeleko, and Mahampha in the Dodoma region of Tanzania.
Mateso (Suffering): Master Musicians of Tanzania, Triple Earth Records Terra CD104, 1989. Compact disc. Recording of Hukwe Zawose (vocals, *zeze*, *mbira*), Lubeleje Chiute, (vocals, *zeze*, *mbira*), and Dickson Mkwama, (vocals, bells, *mbira*). Recorded in London in 1985.
Music from Tanzania and Zanzibar. Caprice Records 21573, 21574, 21577, 1997.

3 compact discs. General compilation providing an overview of traditional and popular music of the mainland and island cultures.

Music of the Farmer Composers of Sukumaland: We Never Sleep, We Dream of Farming, Multicultural Media MCM 3013, 1997. Compact disc. Excellent field recordings and notes by ethnomusicologist Frank Gunderson documenting labor songs and dances of the Sukuma people.

Musiki wa dansi: Afropop Hits from Tanzania. Africassette AC 9403, 1995. Compact disc. Popular dance band music from Tanzania featuring the Orchestra Maquis Original, International Orchestra Safari Sound, Juwata Jazz, and Mlimani Park Orchestra.

Sikinde. Mlimani Park Orchestra. Africassette AC 9402, 1994. Compact disc. Dance band music from Tanzania featuring the Mlimani Park Orchestra band.

Tanzanian Beat. Tatunane. King Record KICC 5221, 1997, Compact disc. Folk and popular Tanzanian music by one of Tanzania's leading bands, Tatunane.

Tanzanie: chants des Wagogo et des Kuria, Maison des Cultures du Monde. Auvidis W 260041, 1992. Compact disc. Wagogo and Kuria songs from Tanzania.

The Art of Hukwe Ubi Zawose: Songs Accompanied by Ilimba and Izeze, JVC World Sounds VICG-5011, 1990. Compact disc. Vocal and instrumental music performed by Hukwe Zawose, Dickson Mkwama, and Lubeleje Chiute.

The Music of Zanzibar. GlobeStyle CDORBD 040, 1990. Compact disc. Taarab music recorded on the island of Zanzibar.

Zanzibar: Music of Celebration. British Library National Sound Archive, International Music Collection, Topic Records TSCD917, 2000. Compact disc. Vocal and instrumental *taarab* and *maulidi* music from Zanzibar from the International Music Collection of the British Library National Sound Archive. Recordings, text, and photographs by ethnomusicologist Janet Topp Fargion

Uganda

Abayudaya: Music from the Jewish People of Uganda. Smithsonian Folkways Recordings 40504. Recordings and text by ethnomusicologist Jeffrey Summit.

Beat the Border. Geoffrey Oryema. Caroline Records, Carol 2333-2, 1993. Compact disc. Recording by internationally popular Ugandan musician, Geoffrey Oryema.

Kikwabanga: Songs and Dances from the Land of Ngaali. Ndere Troupe. Pan Records, PAN 2016CD, 1993. Compact disc. Performances by the Ndere Troupe, sung in various Ugandan languages.

Music from Uganda 1: Traditional; Music from Uganda 2: Modern Traditional Caprice CAP 21495/21553, 1996. Compact discs. Recording of traditional choral, vocal, and instrumental forms of music.

Ngoma: Music from Uganda, Music of the World CDT-142, 1997, prod. Wade Patterson and Bob Haddad. Compact disc. Music from seven of Uganda's ethnic groups, collected as part of the Ngoma Project for cultural preservation.

Ouganda: Aux Sources du Nil, Ocora C560032, 1992. Compact disc. Traditional music of Uganda.

Ouganda: Ensembles villageois du Busoga [Uganda: Village Ensemble of Busoga], Disques VDE-Galloo CD-925, 1997. Compact disc. Traditional village ensembles of Busoga, Uganda.

Ouganda: Musique des Baganda [Uganda: Music of the Baganda People], Ocora C560161 HM 79, 2002. Compact disc. Dance music, songs for religious invocation, and secular songs with percussion, featuring ethnomusicologist Sylvia Nannyonga-Tamusuza

Pearl of Africa Reborn. Samite. Shanachie 65008, 1992. Compact disc. Recording by popular Ugandan musician, Samite.

Royal Court Music from Uganda: 1950 & 1952, Sharp Wood Productions SWP 008/HT 02, 1998. Compact disc. Vocal and instrumental music from Uganda with notes by Andrew Tracey. Recorded in Uganda in 1950 and 1952.

Silina musango. Samite. Xenophile, Xeno 4047, 1996. Compact disc. Recording by popular Ugandan musician, Samite.

Tipu pa Acholi [The Spirit of Acholi]: Songs and Dances of the Acholi in Uganda. Pan Records, PAN 2029CD, 1996. Compact disc. Traditional music of the Acholi people of northern Uganda.

Traditional Music of the Baganda. Evalisto Muyinda. Pan Records, PAN2003, 1991. Compact disc. Traditional music of the Baganda people, as formerly played at the court of the Kabaka of Buganda. Famed musician Evaristo Muyinda plays *ennanga* (harp), *endongo* (lyre), *endingidi* (tubefiddle), *endere* (flute), and *akadinda* and *amadinda* (xylophones).

Watik, Watik: Music from Uganda, Music of the World LAT 50614, 1999. Compact disc. Recording of tradition Ugandan music featuring musician and ethnomusicologist James Makubuya.

Viewing

Options for viewing recorded performances of music, dance, and drama from East Africa are critically limited. The few that are available are often presented out of context and without supporting documentation to make the performances meaningful. Offered below are several available videocassettes of varying quality.

Afrika: Mother of Dance. Ralph Helfer, dir. 1993. (Los Angeles, CA: Red Magic Productions.) Video explores links between African and Arab dance forms, concentrating on different ethnic groups in Kenya.

East African Instruments. 1978. (Lincoln, NE: Great Plains National Instructional Television Library.) Demonstration of instruments from throughout East Africa.

Imbalu: Ritual of Manhood of the Bagisu of Uganda. Richard Hawkins, dir. 1988. (London: Royal Anthropological Institute, University of Manchester, Media Support and Development Centre.) Focuses on the Bagisu *Imbalu* male circumcision ritual in eastern Uganda. is typically performed (to this day) to mark the passage from boyhood to manhood.

Kyekyo: Our Rhythm Goes On. Kayaga Performers. 1996. (Baltimore, MD: Namu Cultural Productions.) Performances of Ugandan traditional music and dance.

Song of the Refugee: A Message of Hope from Africa. PBS Adult Learning Service, 1998. Samite, a musician who fled Uganda in 1982 during the civil wars, returns to Africa. He sings and plays his traditional music.

The JVC/Smithsonian Folkways Video Anthology of Music and Dance of Africa, Volume 3: Kenya, Malawi, Botswana, South Africa. JVC, Victor Company of Japan, 1996. A collection of folk music and dances from Africa. Several segments dedicate to Kenyan musical examples.

The JVC Video Anthology of World Music and Dance, Middle East & Africa II: Egypt, Tunisia, Morocco, Mali, Cameroon, Zaire, Tanzania. JVC, Victor Co. of Japan, 1990. Series of documentary footage of music and dance from the Middle East and Africa documented with supporting text. Section on Tanzania.

Index

∽